ROUND-TRIP TO
DEADSVILLE

AS. SOONE. AS. WEE. TO. BEE. BEGVNNE:
WE. DID. BEGINNE. TO. BEE. VNDONE.

—*English* memento mori *medal, c. 1650*

TIM MATSON

ROUND-TRIP TO DEADSVILLE

A Year in the Funeral Underground

CHELSEA GREEN PUBLISHING COMPANY
White River Junction, Vermont
Totnes, England

Printed in the United States.
First printing September, 2000.

03 02 01 00   1 2 3 4 5

Many of the designations used by manufacturers and sellers to distinguish their products are claimed as trademarks. Where those designations appear in this book and Chelsea Green was aware of a trademark claim, the designations have been printed in initial capital letters.

Library of Congress Cataloging-in-Publication Data
Matson, Tim, 1943—
    Round-trip to deadsville : A year in the funeral underground / Tim Matson.
    p. cm.
    ISBN 1-890132-17-9 hardcover
    ISBN 1-890132-91-8 papercover
    1. Funeral rites and ceremonies—United States. 2. Undertakers and undertaking—United States.

GT3203 .M34 2000
393'.0973—dc21   00-028787

The photograph by Robert E. Pike of Ginseng Willard that appears on page viii belongs to the Pike Archives and is reproduced courtesy of Helen-Chantal Pike. The photograph of the author that appears on page 147 was taken by Joseph Mehling. The quote on page 71 comes from *Northwest Passage,* by Kenneth Lewis Roberts (Garden City, N.Y.: Doubleday, Doran & Co., 1937). The quote on page 84 is from Glennys Howarth's *Last Rites: The Work of the Modern Funeral Director* (Amityville, N.Y.: Baywood, 1996). The quote on page 134 is taken from *Spiked Boots: Sketches of the North Country,* by Robert E. Pike (Woodstock, Vt.: Countryman Press, 1999).

CHELSEA GREEN PUBLISHING COMPANY
Post Office Box 428
White River Junction, VT 05001
(800) 639-4099
www.chelseagreen.com

For Jonathan Matson

Grateful thanks are given to the following people for their help during this project: Ann Aspell, Margo Baldwin, Ted Degener, Marty Mintz, Kathy Hardy Johnson, Helen-Chantal Pike, and Gail Vernazza. Jonathan Matson represented the book and provided invaluable moral support along the way. Special thanks to Stephen Morris, publisher of Chelsea Green, for his practical and creative contributions. I am especially indebted to Jim Schley, my editor, who gave the book inspired attention and guidance throughout, and kept my spirits up when the going got rough. Finally, to the residents of Deadsville, whose generous assistance and considerable kindness made the story possible, my deepest gratitude.

CONTENTS

DARK THOUGHTS Why worry about something you can't do anything about, my friend asked when I mentioned the little problem I was having. We've got to go sometime, what're you saving yourself for?

I tried the usual stuff: counseling, massage, exercise, inspirational reading. I signed up as a deacon at the local church, but the pastor had a nervous breakdown and the police took him away in chains. Not a good omen for religious cures. I tried antidepressants and nearly had a heart attack.

What the hell was happening? There was a time when I was full of piss and vinegar and rarely thought about death. Skydiving, motorcycles, water-ski jumping, logging, roofing—I had an appetite for wild sports and risky jobs. And then, like a tire with a slow leak, I began to lose my nerve. I was trying to get through the Bermuda Triangle of life (a.k.a. my fifties), but I was sinking. Divorce, bills, raising kids, work. No wonder Kazantzakis called this time of life "the full catastrophe." The daily grind was scarier than diving out the door of a jump plane at five thousand feet. My parents were dead, I would be next. I was drinking too much, and the ponds I built for my livelihood looked like graves. A neighbor encouraged me to cheer up. There's light at the end of the tunnel! It sounded like one of those new-age death visions.

Late one winter night sitting by the wood stove, I opened a history of the old logging runs in northern New England. Rober Pike's *Tall Trees,*

Tough Men, a book of northwoods logging lore. Time traveling through these tales of epic river runs, bawdy woodsmen, and teamster gladiators, I thought I could escape. Flipping the pages I stopped at a haunting photograph of George "Ginseng" Willard standing beside an upright coffin. The old logger looked like he was posing for a reshoot of *American Gothic,* with a casket for a wife. Ginseng (he also dug wild herbs) had the grizzled look of an ancient woodchuck. He wore baggy clothes and gave the camera a flinty, fearless gaze. He appeared ready to take on all comers, including the Grim Reaper.

The old man had lived in Guildhall, Vermont, deep in a region known as the Northeast Kingdom, and he'd built the rosewood coffin out of an old dance-hall piano. "My last overcoat," he called it. He slept in it, too. In another shot he wore a wide-brimmed hat and a porcupine-claw necklace, with a Colt revolver in his front pocket. I turned back to the coffin photo. The old man's eyes drilled through me. Something clicked. Death was feeding all my anxiety, and this old timer seemed to be offering a cure. *Build your own coffin.*

Why not? Twenty-five years ago I built my house using a chainsaw and trees from the surrounding woods. I grew most of the food we ate, brewed good beer, dug a swimming pond, and cut firewood for heat. Building a coffin would be the last word in self-sufficiency. Even better, a dose of funereal carpentry might exorcise the death demon, the way homeopathic toxins stimulate the immune system. As the undertakers say, plan ahead.

And so I set off for Deadsville, where I learned that funerals average about five thousand dollars, and dying is pretty much the same can of worms it was when Jessica Mitford exposed the funeral industry in the 1960s. If you want to save your family some money, you've got options to consider. Organ donations, living wills, power of attorney, cemetery plots and headstones, flowers, funeral music, burial or cremation, embalming, perpetual care. There's more to death than building a pine box. I was surprised to find that most cemeteries require burial in an expensive concrete or plastic vault, preventing a natural return to the earth. And did you know that whatever your final wishes, you have no legal rights after you're dead?

I envied Ginseng. Dying must have been simpler back then. Or was it? I began to wonder how his own funeral turned out, and that led me down another path. I made several trips to the Northeast Kingdom, trying to track down Ginseng's descendants, feeling the haunted pull of the northern mountains where I'd first arrived in Vermont more than thirty years ago.

The people who work in the funeral business live in the shadows, shunned by the living. Undertaker, Gravedigger, Coffin Maker . . . we may not admit it, but we think of them as inhabitants of the underworld, colleagues of the Grim Reaper. They are victims of the last taboo—the honest recognition of death. Wouldn't it be more enlightened to welcome these people to the neighborhood?

Why have I chosen to employ their allegorical names, doesn't that perpetuate the stereotype? For one thing, I wanted to protect their privacy and encourage them to be candid about their work without fear of offending patrons past or future. Yet I also saw them as archetypal characters akin to Tarot cards. There's a potency to these characters, an almost supernatural power that overshadows us mere mortals. They are icons in an eternal drama played by interchangeable actors. They are larger than life.

But Deadsville isn't only funeral parlors, graveyards, and morgues. It's also a region of the mind, where arcane beliefs, art, and tradition have as much power as mortuary science, maybe more. I visited the Screenwriter, who wrote some of Hitchcock's best films, including *The Trouble with Harry*, a black comedy about a bungled burial that I believe the director used to quell his own death phobia. I had my chart read by the Astrologer, who showed how the stars shape our attitude to death. I rode an airship with the Balloon Pilot, who sprinkles cremated remains over the Green Mountains. And I listened to the Abenaki's story about coming back from the edge of oblivion with help from his ancestors.

Still, I hadn't built the coffin. Remember Queequeg. When he finished his coffin, the Pequod sank. How long can you wander in Deadsville and hope to get out alive?

And when he had crossed the bridge,
The phantoms came to meet him.

—*Caption scroll from
the silent film* Nosferatu

THE COFFIN MAKER lives on a steep gravel road where the sun to struggles to clear the hills for an hour or two before disappearing again. It's a cold valley with patches of snow that linger into May, the last stop on a nameless road. A hand-lettered sign at the corner says DEAD END. I turn into the driveway, a narrow lane flanked by tall pines, with no room to turn around. One bend after another winds through the trees, and I imagine the Coffin Maker cutting his lumber here under a full moon, a reclusive woodsman hiding away in a forest sprouting coffins. The road plunges deeper into the woods and the trapdoor in my chest opens wide. There's no turning around.

Suddenly the trees open up like a parting curtain to reveal a clearing. There's a house and a vegetable garden and a garage with a basketball hoop over the door. A kid on a ladder is hanging screens on the windows. A black Lab barks at my tires. The air is sweet with apple blossoms. Did I miss a turn?

I get out of the car and give the dog a scratch. A screen door slams. A man in faded jeans and a TROPHY HUSBAND T-shirt walks down the flagstone steps and introduces himself. He clenches a steaming cup of coffee in a shaky hand. There are heavy bags under his eyes, and he squints against the sun. We shake hands, and then he leads me toward his workshop in a closed bay of the gray clapboard garage.

I follow the Coffin Maker through the door, and there it is in the middle of the room resting on two sawhorses, bathed in the soft light of an overhead reflector lamp. The wood has a creamy patina; ripples of grain eddy across the boards. Along each side, three brass handles gleam. Dovetail joints lock the ends together like fingers joined in prayer. The pine box pulls me forward and I reach out and touch the lid. The wood has been sanded and polished to a smooth, waxy finish, and under my hand it feels warm, alive. I run my hand back and forth over the surface.

"It's beautiful," I hear myself say. The Coffin Maker smiles. He tells me how his customers appreciate the simplicity of a traditional design. The coffin is Shaker inspired, put together without nails, using pegs and dovetails, and for Orthodox Jewish customers the brass handles can be omitted, making the coffin one hundred percent kosher. He adds that people also appreciate the seven hundred dollar price, much less than you're likely to find in funeral home showrooms.

"People pay too much for coffins," he says. "They don't plan ahead." He explains that when a family member dies few relatives are in the mood for bargain hunting, and they're easy prey for greedy undertakers. The Coffin Maker commends me for my foresight, suggesting that I could take one of his coffins home today and save the delivery charge.

"I don't want to buy a coffin," I tell him. "I want to learn how to build one."

The Coffin Maker squints, and I imagine his thoughts.

"I'm not going into the coffin business," I reassure him. "I want to build it for myself. I'd like to watch you put one together, learn the basics. I don't want the bottom falling out." I leave out the part about hoping some coffin carpentry will cure my death fear. I don't want him calling the cops.

He puts down the cup. "Give me a hand moving this coffin and you can do more than watch. You can help."

We lift the coffin off the sawhorses and set it down gently on a carpet along the back wall. The sawhorses are also padded with carpeting, a nice touch considering the coffin's destination. I think about old Ginseng and his recycled dance-hall-piano coffin, picturing a lid scarred with cigarette burns and beer-bottle rings. The Coffin Maker reaches up and eases out four pine boards from an overhead rack and I help him lay them out on the sawhorses. He takes another swig of coffee. The bags under his eyes are shrinking and he's moving faster. He picks up a Skilsaw and cuts two of the boards for the sides and then lops off a couple of end pieces. He shows me a handmade jig he's put together to cut the dovetails.

"Kinda looks like a guillotine, doesn't it?" he says, swigging more coffee. By now the puffy wrinkles are gone and he looks ten years younger. This would make a dynamite Folger's commercial.

"Time to offer it up," he whispers. He cuts the dovetails and taps the corners together. "Please, God, I hope it fits." On cue the dovetails lock tight. Then he pulls the joints apart, sands down the pins and tails and hands me a jar of Titebond glue and a toothbrush. "You can help glue the joints."

I carefully spread the glue and then he taps the corners together, using bar clamps to pull them tight. With glue dripping out of the dovetails and bright orange clamps glowing under the reflector lamp, the coffin looks like a patient prepped for surgery. No wonder carpenters are called wood butchers. The Coffin Maker rips two boards for the lid and splices them together using glue, battens, and hardwood pegs. He pounds the square pegs into the round holes drilled in the battens, and they fit snugly. Whoever said you can't fit a square peg in a round hole never built a coffin.

The glue will take time to set, and he asks if I'll give him a lift up the road to get his motorcycle. He left it at a friend's last night.

"Men's group. We had a few beers and I didn't want to kill myself riding home."

We drive a few miles up a mountain road to his friend's, who is presumably nursing a hangover downtown at work. I always wondered what those men's groups were about. The motorcycle is waiting in the garage. A '67 Triumph Bonneville, an English classic. I feel a rush of déjà vu. I rode a Triumph in college, a '66 Daytona 500. I can feel the old ghosts stirring.

The Coffin Maker straddles the bike, pulls the choke, and jumps on the kick starter. After a couple of kicks the machine roars to life. The pipes slap out that sharp staccato beat the Japanese can't touch, and suddenly it's the Sixties again and I'm back in Florida racing through the orange groves with a Confederate blonde breathing down the back of my neck, arms tight around my waist. Hank Ballard and The Midnighters are playing at the beach, and the world is all fresh shrimp and Busch Bavarian and skinny-dipping in the phosphorescent midnight surf.

The Coffin Maker takes off and I tail him back to the shop, and it's like watching myself leaning into the curves, downshifting, burning up the road to my grave. The glue is still tacky, so the Coffin Maker shows me some of his tools, classics like the Bonneville. A small English handsaw that fits his grip perfectly. A Sandvik cabinet scraper with a freshly sharpened blade to smooth down the pine after he's had the boards mechanically sanded. Planes and custom-made jigs, power tools and hand tools scavenged cross-country over the past quarter-century.

"What I like most about building coffins is working with these tools," he says. "They're one of a kind, a combination of utility and beauty. For me that's the essence of the creative process. Usefulness and beauty."

I ask him about the coffins. Doesn't he find them a touch morbid? If it's the tools he enjoys, why this particular line of work? Why not Windsor chairs? He explains that building coffins is just a weekend gig, something he got into by chance. Weekdays he works at a multinational industrial firm, translating operating manuals into foreign languages. He moved to New Hampshire in the hippie days, catapulted from college to backwoods carpentry. One day a friend asked for help building a box. A plain pine box. How could he refuse? After all, this was the back-to-the-land movement. Why buy what you could make yourself?

"Truth is, I'd never heard of home burial," the Coffin Maker recalls. "I'd never even seen a dead body." He did some research, built the coffin, tied it to the top of his VW bug, and drove to Albany, New York. It was New Year's Day and his friend's mother was dead. The family invited him to stay for the ceremony, where her children handled everything, right down to anointing the body with scented oils. They all sat around, told stories, and sang. The next day she was cremated. "It was very moving," he recalls. I ask if he had any regrets at seeing his work go up in smoke. He shakes his head. "Buried or burned, it's a one-way trip."

Eventually the Coffin Maker put on a coat and tie, but over the years that encounter with death grew into a part-time profession, and he now turns out half a dozen coffins annually, polishing his skills, and planning to expand the business when he retires.

"It doesn't spook you?"

He admits that when he began building the coffins, his terror at the thought of death was "a big thing." But word spread, and people began asking for his elegant, low-budget boxes. He decided to take on the Reaper.

"I remember picking up a book by Ray Moody, a study of people who'd had near-death experiences. They all shared memories of a journey toward some kind of light, and a feeling of fearlessness. Our tendency is to fear the unknown, but what I found in my work and reading helped me overcome my fear."

The Coffin Maker checks the dovetails and they're dry. He cuts several lengths of narrow ledgers to fit the bottom of the coffin. "This is the critical part," he says. "This'll keep you from falling out." He shows me how to peg the ledgers around the inside of the coffin floor, then cuts a slab of birch plywood, drops it in, and glues and pegs it down. He packs a handful of hardwood pegs in a plastic baggie and tapes it inside, drops the lid, and tells me that when the time comes, the coffin can be closed with pegs or screws, kosher or non. "I'll put on the finish and the handles tonight," he concludes, dusting off the lid. When I ask him what he uses for a stain, he declines to reveal the formula for his secret blend of sealer and stain, urethane and polish. "Finishing is half the woodworking project. Woodworkers don't give away their finish."

No problem. The woodworking here is way beyond me. I'd be happy to have a box with a bottom that won't drop out. But it does seem a shame that the Coffin Maker's product is so short-lived. I wonder if any of his coffins have found a place this side of the grave, like Ginseng's coffin bed. Occasionally you read about people who buy coffins ahead of time and use them for furniture. A friend of mine knew a college professor who made a glass coffin the centerpiece in his living room, intending to be buried in it like Sleeping Beauty.

The Coffin Maker shakes his head. "I've heard about people using them as wine racks, and I think one of mine is being used as a blanket chest, but most of them don't leave here until there's a death."

"It doesn't bother you that all your craftsmanship is lost?"

"It serves a purpose and it's attractive, that's the point. I usually hear from the family after a service. People call up to thank me. When I hear someone say, Oh, it was beautiful, I know I'm doing the right thing."

The Coffin Maker puts away the bar clamps and the tools. "I like working out here at night," he says, and I don't doubt it. He looks far younger than the old man I saw when I arrived. By nightfall, who knows? "I play my music, refine the process; it's very satisfying." He stops for a moment, as if he were hearing another voice. "My wife thinks it's weird." A shadow passes through the room. "She doesn't like it. She thinks it embarrasses the kids." He picks up the Titebond glue and screws on the cap. What he tells me next would have been tragic anywhere, but in a coffin shop it's stunning. He says that a couple of years ago his oldest son committed suicide. First year of college, away from home, alcohol and depression. He built his son's coffin. He says it helped begin the healing process.

I try to imagine his wife's healing process, watching him build coffins in the garage. The hardest shot the Reaper can dish out, and her husband's in the shop playing undertaker. Weird indeed. Then again, who knows? Maybe the coffins saved them. If the work out here heals the Coffin Maker, if building coffins adds up to comprehending death, if he finds the strength to hold the family together, there might be something to this.

I glance at the coffin lying on the sawhorses awaiting a finish coat, brass handles, and a customer. It's tempting to buy the thing on the spot. Wouldn't it be great to shortcut the healing process for seven hundred bucks? Not a bad deal for peace of mind. But after hearing the Coffin Maker's story, I know shortcuts won't do. Might as well go down to K-Mart and buy a steamer trunk for fifty bucks and call it enlightenment. I don't think Ginseng would be impressed.

On the way home I think about the Coffin Maker's tragedy. He starts out building coffins for a few friends and winds up putting one together for his son. Is coffin building a way to come to terms with death, or is it asking for trouble? I wonder what the Coffin Maker's son thought of his father's workshop sideline? Did this have any effect on his depression? And what goes through the Coffin Maker's head at night? How does someone survive a child's suicide? All I know is that I've met a brave man and I feel ashamed. It makes my troubles seem very small. I'm tempted to wrap up the whole adventure right now. Slap a pine box together and be done. And then it hits me. I know how to build a coffin that won't fall apart, but I have no idea where the damn thing's going to wind up.

THE UNDERTAKER opens the back door of the funeral parlor and strides across the fresh coat of black asphalt to greet me. He's wearing a short-sleeved madras shirt and khakis, with a pager on his belt. The baseball cap on his head says Red Sox. He could pass for a doctor, a lawyer, or a Subaru salesman, but I know who he is and it gives me the creeps. I can't imagine a paycheck fat enough to take a job like this, spending your days picking up dead bodies, embalming corpses, and plotting funerals. Even in our politically correct society, where we're supposed to be tolerant of everyone, this is a prejudice I share with a lot of people. The undertaker is the last guy we allow ourselves to despise.

This revulsion of mine is no doubt a predictable result of standard cultural feeding. Learn your ABC's reading about Oliver Twist's apprenticeship to a gruesome London undertaker, stir in a stew of Gothic horrors by Poe, Stoker, Conan Doyle, and Stevenson, and top it off with a 1950s childhood spent lined up for Saturday matinees like *Them, The Thing,* and *Invasion of the Body Snatchers.* On the way home from the movies we kept our eyes peeled for funeral processions, with their eerie daytime headlights, phantom bright. Passing the town cemetery we held our noses and sang, *The worms crawl in, the worms crawl out, the worms play pinochle on your snout.* . . . Strangest of all, even immersed in that macabre milieu, the grown-ups never mentioned death, which of course made the story even more potent.

Then along came Hitchcock, Polanski, Vietnam, Manson, acid,

Stephen King, punk rock, Jim Jones, and pretty soon everybody's wearing black. You'd think the undertaker would become a folk hero, but in America we prefer death at a televised remove. Everybody wants to go to heaven but nobody wants to die.

D RIVING HOME from the Coffin Maker's, I knew there would be more to this healing process than getting hold of a pine box. I could build a coffin, fill it with red wine or blankets, or sleep in it like old Ginseng, but one day it would close for good. And I had no idea how I wanted to be disposed of. So many options. Interred. Committed to the sea. Buried. Scattered. Sprinkled. Composted. Frozen. Melted. Compacted. Invested. Worshipped. Forgotten. Memorialized. Pulped. Shredded. You can't just walk off into the woods like an Indian. The bill for search and recovery could wipe out your IRA. No, the motto of the funeral industry is Plan Ahead, and they're not kidding.

I need a disposal plan, and I figure the Undertaker can lay out the choices. He operates out of a small-town funeral home, and recently buried one of my neighbors. For the last ten years of her life she'd lived on Social Security and gathered beer cans and bottles alongside the road, not to Keep Vermont Green mind you, but to save up for her funeral. Fifty bucks a month, she told me proudly, never missed a payment until the five grand was paid off. I wonder if some of the cans she retrieved wound up recycled in her baby-blue, stainless-steel coffin, where she rested at the church service, jacked up on a gurney at the back of the sanctuary. The coffin was a Greek Revival mini-mausoleum with swing handles, layers of lintels, Doric columns embossed on the corners, and a black rubber gasket to keep out the water and the worms. I admired her, making all those payments, confident that there was a plot for her beside her husband under a granite headstone a whole lot more durable than the trailer they'd lived in. Sure, she'd have been better off earning interest on the funeral money, but making payments to the undertaker is an Appalachian tradition. The dividend, they say, is peace of mind.

Cremation is not an option for most of the old timers I know. They want to go the way of their parents and grandparents, before the coming of the oven. They'd been stubborn enough to hang onto their hard-scrabble fields after most farmers with any sense moved west. A lifetime pulling granite boulders and digging post holes and cellars and wells had acquainted them intimately with the earth. A cold hole in the ground looks much more natural to a Vermonter than a furnace. Damned if they'd let the wind blow them away now.

I don't have that tradition behind me. My grandparents came over from Norway and Ireland, I'd never met them, and I had no idea if they were buried, burned, embalmed, or entombed. Before my father died, he said he wanted his ashes scattered in the Atlantic off his home in Montauk. But with five children living hither and yon around the country, the commitment kept getting postponed. Years passed. The house was on the market but it didn't sell. Then my mother died, and I took her ashes and buried them in a flower garden in front of my house. I couldn't take two unsettled spirits haunting me. Finally, seven years after he died, we gathered to scatter Dad's ashes in the surf. A few weeks later the house sold.

I don't want to linger around in that kind of afterlife limbo. Everybody's heard about the ashes in the closet nobody bothered to scatter, and undertakers frequently complain about being left with "cremains" nobody wants to pick up. I read about a pilot in California who made a fortune supposedly scattering ashes over the Pacific. One day he skipped town, leaving a warehouse full of remains behind. That's a lot of restless souls to account for. He wound up committing suicide. Even immediate ash disposal might go awry. In some states, full disclosure statements are required to sell real estate. Does that include ashes in the flower garden? Could Mom's ashes jinx a sale? If I move, do I dig her up and take her along? Is this a ploy to sell cemetery plots?

I follow the Undertaker toward the door. The funeral home is a ranch-style building with a hip roof. It could be anybody's house, except for the discreet sign out front, the church next door, and the graveyard across the street. It must be fun giving directions.

The Undertaker leads me through the back door into a large carpeted room with wooden chairs against the walls, facing front and center. I wonder who will be next. We sit next to a throbbing air conditioner, and he asks how he can help. I tell him I've been thinking about my funeral plans. He asks me if I have any preferences, and I admit that I've been thinking about building my own coffin. He nods. "I did a service not long ago for a family that built their father's casket. They owned a saw-mill, so I guess it seemed like a natural thing to do."

Is he suggesting that if you don't own a sawmill, it's unnatural to build a coffin? I've heard that these guys are good salesmen. I tell him I have to decide what happens after I'm, well, inside. It boils down to cremation or burial, right?

"More or less," he nods. "But before you decide, I like to get the whole family involved. A lot of this is about making sure the survivors are satis-fied. There's an old saying, *Funerals are for the living.*"

I explain that I'm divorced and my main concern is not wasting money my kids could use later on.

"But if price were no object, what would you want?"

I tell him my parents were cremated and that seems like an option, not that it doesn't have some disadvantages.

"Go on," he says gently, like a therapist.

"Well, what about the gas? It does use gas, doesn't it?"

"Propane," he nods.

"How much?"

"It depends on the person, how big they are." He pauses, running an appraising eye over me. "I'd say you'd need about thirty gallons."

Thirty gallons! I could run my house for a month on thirty gallons. There must be thousands of people going up in smoke every day, burn-ing up fossil fuels and fouling the atmosphere. I'd always assumed that cremation was the environmentally friendly alternative to burial. After all, we can't go on forever filling the land with cemeteries, there won't be room left for the living. But at thirty gallons a corpse, what about ashes rain?

He admits he never considered it. Then he whips out a funeral home contract, pointing out the basic cremation package, which includes body removal, transportation to the crematorium, funeral service arrangements, family conference, legal paperwork, and placement of the obituary. Total cost $1,350, including a cardboard coffin, with the option to use my own coffin, which won't save me a dime.

The alternative is burial in a cemetery, and now it gets complicated fast. The problem is the body. It has to be moved around, from place of death to funeral home to cemetery, with optional stops in between, at the funeral service and perhaps a storage vault. Unless it's buried within forty-eight hours or so, the body needs to be embalmed to prevent decay, adding more to the cost. A cemetery plot has to be purchased. There's a charge for opening the grave. There might be an extra charge for "perpetual care" to insure that the grave will be maintained. Plus a bunch of fine-print fees for the use of equipment for a memorial service in church or elsewhere, use of equipment and staff for graveside services, even cosmetology. Cemetery burial appears to run at least three thousand bucks, not including the coffin.

"It costs twice as much to get buried as burned?"

"Roughly."

I thought about my parents' low-budget cremations, which hadn't been chosen to save money. They could have bought cemetery plots and headstones. But where? They'd worked in Manhattan, moved to the suburbs, divorced, moved several times, never really becoming part of a community. The children of immigrants, they too were rootless. On the other hand, I'd been part of a small-town community for a quarter century. I could imagine a stone in my hometown graveyard, descendants visiting occasionally. It might give them a sense of continuity I never had. I thought about my neighbors, with parents lying in family plots in the small cemeteries around these hills. I'd moved to Vermont to be part of a rural tradition. Wasn't ending up in a graveyard part of that tradition?

The phone rings and the Undertaker steps into his office to take the call. I think about my parents and all the people I've known who wound up in a cardboard box, left behind in closets and funeral homes, scattered in the ocean, dusted on flower gardens and golf courses. Our disposable economy has progressed from packaging products to packaging our parents. We stick them in nursing homes and shove them in cremation ovens. It's a good way to save money, conserve open space, and best of all, you don't have to think about the choices. No coffins and headstones and graveyards to consider, ignore death until it hits. Just bake and shake, very liberating. But if we're all so enlightened, why all the depression and anxiety? Perhaps, down deep, the white worm doesn't like being ignored.

When the Undertaker gets off the phone I ask about the coffins. No sign of them anywhere.

"We prefer calling them caskets," he says defensively.

"Is there a difference?"

"Two different shapes. Early coffins were six-sided, the old mummy shape. They flared out at the shoulders, then tapered down to the feet. They also called them toe pinchers. They were handmade, often measured exactly to fit the deceased." He says that during the industrial revolution as the economy switched to mass production, it became more efficient to make a rectangular box. About the same time, the funeral industry was getting established, and a rectangular box seemed less frightening to clients. The less it looked like a body, the less it spooked people. So they got rid of the old shape and the nasty old word, and sales went up.

Forget "coffin," with its ghoulish shape and gloomy associations. Say the word and you can hear grandpa's death rattle, not to mention the unfortunate association with cigarettes. Coffin nails, indeed. Some of our best customers are smokers! No wonder the funeral industry prefers the word caskets. A tisket a casket, soothing as a nursery rhyme. Could it be that our denial of death has less to do with existential dread than savvy marketing?

I follow the Undertaker down a thickly carpeted stairway to the basement Casket Viewing Room. About halfway down the stairs I notice a sour chemical odor. Embalming fluid. The Undertaker hasn't put as much money into his ventilating system as his driveway pavement. We pass through a small foyer into a crowded, windowless display room full of coffins. The coffins lie on shelves along the walls and on a raised stage in the middle of the room. Most of them are steel, a few made of highly polished hardwood, all with elaborate swing handles. Most are closed, but a few are open to reveal padded interiors covered with ruffled white linen and thick pillows. On these, the lids are split, like horizontal Dutch doors, with the lower half closed. When I look inside I see that the mattress goes only below the open section of lid.

"You can order a full couch if you like," the Undertaker quickly explains. "But the half-couch option does offer a significant saving." He doesn't have to add that nobody really expects the occupant to notice the difference. There are price tags on the coffins, and they range from $1,500 to as much as $4,000 for an elaborate steel sarcophagus that features a frilly full-length couch, including a fully upholstered lid, which creates the unsettling impression of a pillow that would suffocate the occupant upon closing.

At the far end of the room is an arrangement of coffins with a more utilitarian look. No sculptured lintels, no frescos, no Greek corner columns. The prices are significantly lower. I also notice that they have no handles. Another price-cutting feature?

"No, those are vaults," the Undertaker explains.

"Vaults?"

"To reinforce a coffin. Coffins don't last forever, they rot or rust, and then the ground collapses. Last year a backhoe working in the town cemetery fell in a hole. Vaults prevent the ground from caving in. They've got a concrete core, with a decorative plastic finish. Most cemeteries require them."

"You have to put one coffin inside another coffin?"

He nods.

There goes the wholesome alternative to cremation. How can you return to the food chain in a concrete hazardous-waste bunker? The Undertaker must sense my concern because he suggests another option. Cremation first, then burial in a small urn.

"No vault?"

"No vault."

I tell him I'll think about it.

There's a door near the vault display. I look inside and discover a small room jammed with a few more coffins. One, a crude wooden job with unsanded edges and rope handles, and another, suffocating purple, of indeterminate material. They're tagged at $500 each.

"What's this one made of?" I ask, pointing to the purple coffin.

"Oh, some kind of particle board. Not very appealing, but I do have to keep something for people with a low budget. I don't even stock them at our funeral home up north."

He tells me that the funeral home is a family operation, and they also operate a parlor in one of the state's big cities, with a large French Canadian and Italian population. "The people up there are more ethnic," he says. "It's a big family deal, fancy funerals, striped upholstery in the coffins. Everybody who comes to a funeral gets taken out to dinner after. Down here it's mostly WASPS who are extremely frugal and afraid of death. After the funeral it's back to the house for finger sandwiches and punch."

I'd be afraid of death too, if I could only afford a purple coffin. Perhaps they eat sandwiches and finger food so they can afford something nicer.

I follow the Undertaker upstairs and we walk outside. The day is still heating up, and the parking lot is close to bubbling. I ask him where he keeps the hearse, wondering if it's gone the way of the toe-pincher and the black mourning band. It turns out that he hides it behind closed doors in the garage attached to his house, next to the parking lot. No point upsetting anybody by parking it outside, could be bad for business.

Neighbors might not like the sight of a hearse in the parking lot, but when I was younger, they were cool. I remember visiting a friend at Harvard who'd just bought a secondhand hearse. It had a stovepipe sticking through the roof, and a woodstove inside. He used it for weekend ski trips to Vermont. It even had a name: Brunhilda.

As the Sixties picked up steam, you'd see hearses on college campuses, usually repainted in day-glo rainbows, slathered with psychedelic stickers. They were great for crosscountry traveling and, of course, sex. You don't see many used hearses around today, thanks to the death-denial of the past few decades. I hear you can hardly give away a used hearse, which is a shame because they're steel-cage reinforced, tougher than SUVs, and they scare other drivers out of the way.

The Undertaker's hearse, a Cadillac modified by Superior Coach, features a removable plastic sign panel on the front grill: ƎƆИA⅃UᙠMA.

"What's that?"

"It's 'ambulance,' mirror image, to get people to pull over."

The Undertaker explains that he also runs an ambulance service, doubling the use of the hearse, which otherwise would be gathering dust between death removals. I don't know how eager I'd be to have a hearse haul me away after a heart attack.

Near the hearse lies a flattened and stained cardboard box with the words HUMAN REMAINS printed on the side. I take a step closer and notice the word HEAD at one end.

"Coffin?"

"No, it's an air tray. They're used to ship bodies. We get a lot of folks coming back home from Florida."

An extreme way to get more leg room on the plane.

The Undertaker's pager beeps and he clicks it off.

"My brother will get it."

I ask him how he and his brother got into the business. He says his father started the funeral home after coming back from World War II. "I grew up in the business, helping my father, and after he put me through college I was on my own. I asked myself what I knew how to do, and this was it." Later on his brother joined him, and they alternate being on call.

He says the hours are rough. People don't die on a nine to five schedule, they tend to go in the early hours of the morning, late at night, after big holiday dinners, jogging after work, shoveling snow on the weekends, having sex. More people die in the winter than other seasons, and in Vermont that makes undertaking a hazardous occupation.

"One of the toughest things about this business is making a death call at Thanksgiving or Christmas. In the middle of dinner. Or I might be at a baseball game with my son. It used to be that somebody always had to be at home near the phone and know where Dad was. If he was out for dinner, we'd have to call. Pagers make it a little better now, but that doesn't make it any easier on my kids."

So the funeral home really is a home after all, not just a euphemism for the morgue. It's a place where kids grow up with chemical smells and dead bodies and an endless procession of grieving customers. Where death is the rule, not the exception. Where you get used to midnight calls and heartbroken strangers. Where death becomes so commonplace that one day you step into your father's shoes.

"It's a cultural thing," he says. "People in this business tend to grow up in it. But I love the work because I get a lot of positive feedback. After all, people are extremely grateful. Up north especially, you're seen as a vital part of the community." He pauses and the enthusiasm fades. "Down here it's different. I know parents who won't let their kids go to a funeral, even a fifteen-year-old kid. Sometimes we have open houses, educational programs. Kids come here from high school to visit and they're scared to go in the casket display room. It kills me how afraid people are of death. People don't want to face it. Europeans aren't afraid."

The Undertaker hands me a contract and I tell him I'll think about it. At home I practice thinking like a European but that doesn't help. I fall asleep and dream about being buried alive in a purple coffin.

THE GRAVEYARD GUIDE is late, but folding chairs have been set up on the lawn facing the mausoleum, so we sit down sheepishly and wait for the tour to begin. It's a hot Sunday afternoon in August and the grass between the headstones is parched and brittle. Except for a couple of kids playing hide-and-seek between the graves, we're a solemn audience of white-haired elders. This is supposed to be an historical tour of the town cemetery, which features several prominent former residents and a fine view overlooking the village green, but it feels unnervingly like a gathering of tire-kickers.

The guide arrives and introduces herself, although most of us already know her as the unofficial town historian, a British expatriate with a bloodhound's instinct for the obscure particulars of Vermont village history. I have the impression that she feels protective about New England, like a nervous parent watching a child step out into the world.

This big, brooding mausoleum is the final resting place for a famous town ancestor who made a fortune in dry-goods, then went on to spend twenty-five years in the U.S. Senate during the mid-nineteenth century. When he retired, he built a pink Gothic-revival palace in the middle of town and, just before he died, this twenty-foot-high granite tomb to enshrine himself, his wife, and their children. From the base of its graceful Ionian columns to the top of the massive vaulted roof, it's a miniature Greek temple, which as the Graveyard Guide points out, suggests a change in the Senator's taste, if not an improvement.

The Graveyard Guide doesn't know how much the Senator spent on the tomb, but the logistics are epic. Huge granite blocks dynamited out of the quarries in Barre, Vermont, transported by rail to a town ten miles to the west of here, and then hauled over the mountain by a team of two dozen horses. The capstone alone weighed twenty tons and was too heavy to drag, even over snow, so it had to be hoisted onto a capstan and pulled forward one end at a time. When the first one didn't fit, another had to be blasted out of the quarry and hauled in. A north-country *Fitzcarraldo.*

The sun blazes down and I'm almost envious of the Senator and his family chilling out in the naturally air-conditioned tomb, but otherwise it's a pretentious example of graveyard overkill. I know there's an ancient tradition of grandiose tomb building that goes back to the pyramids, but those ventures were fueled by a religious belief in the afterlife. However, this mausoleum offers no epitaphs, no farewells, no spiritual platitudes, no dates, which creates a curiously unfinished impression, as if the old Senator might be stuck in time somewhere, neither dead nor alive. Being entombed above ground adds to the impression of suspended animation. Or is that the point? *Hell no, we won't go!*

The Graveyard Guide leads us away from the mausoleum to the smaller graves down the hill, where weathered headstones evoke a more sympathetic sensation of shared humility in the face of death. She points out various stones, some dating back two centuries, and then recounts the graveyard's origin. A child had died in the village and her mother feared for her security in the existing, more remote town cemetery. Grave robbers roamed the hills then, digging up valuables traditionally buried with the deceased, and medical students from a local college showed up at night seeking cadavers. The woman begged the town fathers to allow the child to be buried on a nearby hill so she could watch the grave from her kitchen window. The request was approved, and every night she lit a lamp on the grave to keep her vigil. A child dies and a graveyard is born.

We weave through the old graves, picking up lessons in geology as well as town history. Slate slabs were easier to quarry than granite, but they haven't held up as well. Some of them are flaking apart, their letter-ing eroded and illegible. A couple of slate headstones have peaked tops with lead caps to protect against the rain. They look like little houses. Many of the slate markers are adorned with delicately carved weeping willows, a popular nineteenth-century gravestone motif. The Graveyard Guide leads us to a soapstone marker, which has fared little better than the slate. Here another common icon, a funeral urn, is eroding into ghostly oblivion. Our guide takes a step closer and points out a small word, faintly visible. URN, it says, with an arrow pointing at the design.

"I'd wager that the carver transferred the artist's sketch onto the stone, design instructions and all." The Graveyard Guide smiles, pleased with her detective work.

The quest for immortality, botched in stone.

Nearby is a more durable granite marker identified with the name Richardson. It starts off impressively enough, letters tall and proud, but as the name marches along the artist begins to run out of space. The letters shrink down until SON is just that, a Lilliputian miniature of the original font. More of the urn carver's handiwork? Was he an amateur, a lush, or the only guy in town with a stonecarving chisel? And what hap-pened when the stones were planted? Did the survivors run him out of town, demand their money, or slap him on the back and head for the tavern? There's a mystery here with an endless supply of plots, and I get a taste of our guide's pleasure at unearthing these graveyard puzzles.

She steers us toward an orderly line of granite stones, all young men according to their biographical dates, all dead the same year. The Grave-yard Guide tells us that they were soldiers. "Volunteers for the Civil War," she says, "and they never got past training camp. They all died of diphtheria. You see, these were boys who'd never been out of Vermont before, never exposed to outside germs." The tragedy of war and disease couldn't be more eloquent than this long line of silent stones.

We meander through two hundred years of town history, noting how one married couple's *his* and *hers* stones had cracked in exactly the same place; musing on the intentions of a triple widower planted with all three wives—wondering if that meant bad luck, polygamy, three-way necrophilia, or murder. We pass several headstones with a carving of a hand, finger pointing up, and the popular farewell, "Gone Home." There are indications of infant deaths, wholesale family catastrophes, and a couple of centenaries. One couple's stone includes the deceased husband's birth and death dates, next to the wife's year of birth and the number 19 followed by a blank. The Y2K problem wasn't limited to computers.

We crawl around on all fours trying to decipher footstones, rub lichen off eroded soapstone, and chat about town history, until we encounter a fellow with a message from the grave. *Stranger, as you are now so once was I / As I am now so will you be.* I try to imagine myself planted on this hillside, settling down where my kids might come now and then, not so much to mourn their father, but to know that he had been part of a community, and was still. Would it give them a sense of roots? Or was this just another irrational vanity, slighter than the Senator's, but equally silly?

A COUPLE OF DAYS LATER I phone the graveyard commissioner to inquire about booking myself a space, but he's out of town. That gives me some time to dig into the history of cemeteries, and ponder why a once popular tradition has fallen so far out of fashion. Few of my friends have expressed interest in cemetery burial, and the percentage of new graves in the town cemetery is low.

Much of the credit for the demise of cemetery burials goes to Jessica Mitford. In 1963 she published *The American Way of Death,* a scorching critique of the funeral industry, which had been gouging bereaved customers for decades. In the late 1950s and early 1960s, the average funeral was one of the top three purchases in America, right up there with a house and a car. Along came Mitford, demonstrating that everything funereal was obscenely overpriced, if not downright unnecessary, from coffins and headstones to "burial footwear." She cited insider trade journals and recounted visits to funeral homes, cemeteries, and florists, where she played the part of grieving survivor. Invariably, they all tried to rip her off. She questioned the need for instant embalming, and quoted physicians who backed her up. She exposed predatory business methods, including coffin displays arranged like the one I'd seen, where a shabby knock-off was used to frighten people into more expensive purchases. She cited overpriced and, in her opinion, unnecessary vaults; schemes to cheat survivors benefiting from generous insurance policies; overcharges after industrial disasters; and the promotion of "preneed" payments whereby people pay ahead of time for services that might not be available when the time comes. Such as paying for a funeral in Vermont and dropping dead in Hawaii. And who can guarantee that the funeral home will still be in business decades down the road? Even if the plan works out, why donate the interest money to the funeral home?

Incredible as it may seem, thirty-six years after publication of her book many of the same practices still exist, enough in fact to have justified a revised edition in 1998, revealing overpriced coffins and vaults, deceptive contracts, and unethical connections between undertakers, churches, and cemeteries. The average price of a funeral in the United States is now roughly $5,000, a substantial percentage of which often comes as a surprise to bereaved survivors.

Mitford discouraged preneed purchases, as do most consumer advocates today, although waiting until a death occurs can also put survivors in a vulnerable position. As one national cemetery association executive told me, "When your mind is ablaze with grief, you may walk out of a funeral home without remembering a single thing you just signed for." Mourners don't make particularly astute buyers, and the funeral industry knows that. Consumer advocates recommend planning ahead without paying ahead.

When the commissioner of the town graveyard calls back, he says that a ten-by-thirteen plot costs $500, including "perpetual care," which sounds like a bargain for an eternity of lawnmowing and weeding. As it turns out, each plot has room for four vaults, or "a whole lot of cremation urns." I hadn't thought about additional spaces. It gives me a chill to realize the grave I'm considering as a visiting place for my kids would have room for them, too.

THE STONE CARVER looks as if he's weathered the years well. It's been more than two decades since I've seen him and he's gone gray, but he grips the heavy pneumatic drill at eye level, chipping out a crown of thorns, and his biceps stretch the sleeves of his T-shirt tight. He wears protective goggles and ear guards, and a cigarette smolders between his lips. Though the drill pounds away like a machine gun, he manages to work the tip with the precision of a scalpel, oblivious to the noise, the vibration, and the buzz of the suction hose swallowing up the chips, dust, and smoke. He hasn't seen me come into the shed, and I don't want to break up his flow, so I wander around, heeding his earlier warning to watch my step.

The granite shed is a beat-up, brown wooden hanger secluded at the end of a rusty railroad spur in the old riverside industrial section of Barre, Vermont. It's long and low, like an old coffin that should have been buried well before now. It's huge, over a hundred yards in length, dimly lit, and loud. I sneak in through a side door, as the Stone Carver suggested, to avoid going through the small front office and triggering a shutdown.

This is not a place for tourists. Men wearing overalls, jumpsuits, canvas aprons, and rubber boots hustle huge blocks of granite from one end to the other, turning what was once a mountain of molten lava into progressively smaller rectangles and cubes and slants, moving them from tall, screaming, diamond-tipped saws through whirling polishing stones, finally into the hands of the carvers and sandblasters, who sculpt the biographical dates, famous last words, and images. Loads of granite thunder overhead strapped beneath speeding hydraulic cranes that block out the light as they go by, halting work below until the eclipse passes.

The floor is a shadowed maze of wooden pallets, unfinished headstones, wet gutters, and wires. It's a huge pinball game, air hammers and shrieking saws, flashing lights, and careening boulders. I work my way to the north end of the shed, passing a sculptor hand-chiseling a ten-foot-tall grizzly bear. Past stone angels, saints, the Virgin Mary, and a fireman's granite hat. A man in dusty overalls uses a hammer and cat's-paw to uncrate slabs of polished Indian granite: dazzling reds, blacks, and browns. Behind a glass wall, headstones are being masked with rubber stencils and sandblasted. In the middle of this frenzy, it's easy to forget why everyone is here. Perhaps stone does conquer death.

At four o'clock the machines shut down and people pack their lunch boxes and tools to go home, or wherever you go after a day making gravestones. I catch up with the Stone Carver. He shows me the memorial he's working on, a headstone with a bas-relief of Christ wearing his horrible crown. It's a traditional memorial design, ECCE HOMO—*Behold the Man.* The name of the deceased will be sandblasted under the carving.

"I could do one for you," the Stone Carver suggests with a smile, but I shake my head, suggesting something a bit lighter. In fact, I'm not sure I want a gravestone of any kind, but as I told him earlier, I'm on a strange sort of quest, and not ruling out any options. I told him about my visit to the town cemetery, and its appealing graveyard tradition. I figured he'd understand. Confront mortality, overcome death, leave a legacy with a little style. "Everybody must get stoned, right?" he laughs.

The Stone Carver and I met during the gold rush of the early 1970s when Vermont beckoned like the Big Rock-Candy Mountain to artists, writers, deserters, and ice-cream makers. He'd been a sculpture student in New York City, moved to Vermont to work in local theatre, got married and had a couple of kids, divorced, and wound up in the sheds. If you want to make a living as a sculptor in Vermont, he told me, carving headstones is about the only way to go. The paychecks are reliable, even if working anonymously does shortchange the ego.

BARRE IS THE monument capital of the United States, built on a volcanic mountain of the high-quality granite discovered nearly two hundred years ago in the south end of town. Much of the stone is fine-grained and rich in silica, which yields well to carving and polishing. It's far more durable than marble, slate, or soapstone, and ideal for public and private memorial sculpture. Lesser grades are excellent for building materials, landscaping, and industrial manufacturing, including the twenty-ton paper rollers that likely had a part in producing the paper you now hold in your hands.

One hundred years ago Barre was a boomtown with a population unlike any other in Vermont. The quarries had been worked first by early colonists from Scotland, who produced grindstones for the mills that helped New England gain economic independence. In 1875, the Barre Railroad No. 1 ran a spur into town, and business for larger stones took off. The highly prized granite attracted immigrant stone carvers from Scandinavia, Lebanon, and most famously, Italy. Experienced sculptors from Carrara and Milan, Italy's two prominent stone-cutting regions, came to Barre and helped build the many quarries and processing sheds that made the famous "City of the Dead." Between 1880 and 1894, Barre's population shot up to ten thousand, a five-fold increase, and every week a new house was started. Black-powder explosions echoed from the quarries, the sheds roared, horsedrawn sleds and wagons pounded the streets, and railroad cars drummed down the tracks loaded with the disappearing mountains.

Many observers saw a grand future for Barre, and one commentator confidently predicted, "Barre is destined to become, in the not too distant future, the metropolis of the state." Driving through Barre today, it's clear that things didn't pan out so grandly. Following the Stone Carver's directions to the shed, I had to drive through a maze of narrow potholed streets, one-way underpasses, and abandoned railroad crossings. Barre feels like a town that put itself together in a frenzy, high times and hangovers preserved shoulder to shoulder, magnificent memorials beside forlorn sheds, low-income housing crowding Victorian mansions.

No doubt the incoherent city layout was due to fast expansion and jumbled ethnic aesthetics, but I wonder if there wasn't a darker force at work. The town's name suggests a macabre destiny—"Get Buried in Barre." If a clue to the town's fate as the capital of American gravestones lay in its name, tragedy was embedded in the stone itself. The silica that gave the granite its highly polishable character also lodged in the workers' lungs, often leading to silicosis or tuberculosis, and early death.

Immigrant carvers were accustomed to working with a more forgiving Italian marble, in better ventilated workshops. But for many months of the year the Barre sheds were shut tight against the cold, while water was used to cool the cutting blades and keep down the dust. The combination of silica and the damp cold was a killer. Early residents of Barre described stone cutters walking home from the sheds covered with white dust from head to toe, like ghosts. It wasn't until the 1930s that ventilation systems were installed to remove the dust, and by then several generations of granite cutters had died painful, premature deaths. One street after another became known as *La Strada delle Vedove,* street of widows, where the surviving women ran boarding houses and sold *grappa,* a bootleg liquor distilled from homemade wine.

"The stone will kill you," the Stone Carver remembers being told by a shed owner who rented him his first working space. What about the ventilation ducts? I ask. He shrugs. It wasn't only the dust, there were the thundering overhead cranes, capillary-shattering pneumatic drills, and the slippery, rubble-strewn floors. I thought about the fatalistic stone carver in Mari Tomasi's novel *Like Lesser Gods,* set in Barre before World War II. The carver has seen most of his fellow workers die of silicosis, his wife harangues him to quit the sheds for the sake of his family, yet he stays. "I love the stone," is his humble explanation.

The Stone Carver suggests a trip to Hope Cemetery, the graveyard where many of Barre's finest memorials can be seen. It's an uphill ride from the industrial riverside to a slope overlooking town. We pass between two stately granite guardians representing Peace and Salvation, and the cemetery appears, an attractively landscaped last stop for more than six thousand souls. The memorials include staunch mausoleums, lofty obelisks, symbolically broken columns, statues, and carvings that range from classical pietàs, angels, and saints to a soccer ball, a biplane, and an overstuffed chair commissioned by a granite-company owner who wanted his grave to offer tired visitors a place to rest. A touching gesture, although I have sat in more comfortable chairs.

In spite of the miscellaneous carving styles, the cemetery has a pleasing, unified appearance because the stones are all Barre gray granite. Another integrating element is the frequent use of "pitch-rock" carving, which gives the stone a rugged, unfinished look, unlike the classic European polish. Pitch-rock designs require a labor-intensive, highly skilled technique no longer practiced, making the cemetery even more unusual.

As we walk among the monuments and headstones, the Stone Carver tells me that Barre's half-dozen cemeteries were not exclusively used for funeral interments and mournful visits. They were also the Sunday picnic grounds for stone carvers, quarrymen, and their families, who gathered to play music, drink homemade wine, and admire the newest sculptures. The cemeteries became the immigrants' beloved parks, and a link to their European roots, where funerary cults and graveyard gatherings had been popular and even fashionable.

The Stone Carver leads me to a large sculpture of a dying stone carver and his grieving wife. He recounts the story of Louis Brusha, a notable carver who died of silicosis sixty years ago. Anticipating his death, he designed the memorial as a tribute to his beloved wife and a life dedicated to the stone. After Brusha's death, it was executed by a fellow carver. With a sly grin the Stone Carver notes the erotic contours of the woman's hips under the folds of her gown, a tribute to the carver's skills, and perhaps his hankerings for the widow.

"He designed his own stone?" I ask, and the Stone Carver nods.

He leads me to several more monuments designed and often carved by the men now beneath them. Giuseppi Donati's monument is a surreal composition showing the sculptor as a young man wearing an Italian police officer's uniform during World War II. As he enjoys a cigarette and daydreams, the smoke rises into an ethereal image of the woman he loves, his future wife. Nearby, Albert Ceppi's headstone is a self-portrait of the sculptor at work, pneumatic drill in hand, goggles over his eyes. Donatto Coletti, a Barre sculptor and art teacher, designed his own headstone with an inset bronze medallion to commemorate his long marriage. I would later find many more memorials throughout Barre, from streetside obelisks to cemetery mausoleums, created by those they memorialize. Perhaps building your own coffin isn't so strange after all.

A light rain begins to fall from a gray sky that matches the granite on the hill. We ignore the rain and keep walking. The Stone Carver points out a headstone framed by a vine of carved roses, icons of eternal love. He touches the delicately etched petals, which stand out in lifelike relief from the stone, and tells me that few carvers today have the skill or the time for the old chiaroscuro style. Most work is now done by sandblasters, and as he shows me on another stone, the results are perfunctory and flat. It appears that headstone carving is truly a dying art.

I ask the Stone Carver if he will chisel his own monument. He shakes his head.

"I've carved a lot of stone. If my kids want to remember me, they know where to look." He glances around the cemetery. "I think it's pretty silly, all this wasted space."

"If I wanted a stone," I ask, "what would it cost?"

The Stone Carver says he has no idea. He explains that the business has been transformed into assembly-line production. Brokers bring him jobs, he makes a bid, and if he wins, the stone is delivered and he executes the carving. The lettering and polishing is done by someone else, and then the finished stone goes out. He gets paid for his work only. He adds that it's not the kind of business where you get much feedback from your customers.

I decide not to ask him why he spent the last twenty years filling up graveyards if he thinks it's a silly idea, but I get the answer anyway. We've been wandering through the tombstones and the talk has turned to raising kids, surviving divorce, and making it as an artist.

"Living, not dying, that's the hard part," he says, lighting another cigarette. "After the divorce, it was the work that saved me. Getting up in the morning, going to the sheds, carving the stone. It was the routine that got me through. The stones are for the living."

I thought about the Coffin Maker surviving his son's suicide by putting together pine boxes in his shed, and Ginseng Willard sleeping in his homemade coffin, living to a ripe old age. I remembered the Undertaker's story about paying his way through college by embalming corpses in the family basement. Funerals are for the living, he too had said. It sounded like a merchandising cliché the first time I heard it, but here was the Stone Carver saying the same thing. *The stones are for the living.* I thought about the odyssey I'd embarked upon, and realized that I was beginning to feel differently about death. The mortal fear was turning into something else, something less terrifying and alien. I was learning my way around the neighborhood.

THE LAWYER runs a one-man show in a small Vermont town, and today one of his clients shot up a No Parking sign in a wildlife preserve and wound up in shackles in a maximum-security lockup, so we haven't got much time before he's charging off to court. Last week we were in family court together for the final hearing on my divorce, and with that settled, I'm in his office to revise my Last Will and Testament and give him a bottle of Dutch vodka.

Unlike most attorneys I've known, the Lawyer is an unembarrassed hired gun, and very smart. He's also my age, with years in the military and a divorce under his belt, and kids. We've got stuff in common. Remarkably, his fees are also reasonable. The trade-off is that he smokes like a dragline gobbling up buckets of intoxicating mud, which drives me nuts. I don't give a damn about second-hand smoke, I only wish I had a vice that gave me as much obvious pleasure. I'd love to light up a Camel and listen to his mind-boggling monologues all afternoon, but I gave up coffin nails years ago, dreaming of immortality.

It doesn't take long to rewrite the will. Beneficiaries, executor, trustee. There's something admirably democratic about a will. It works equally well for two bucks or two million. The curious thing is how cool-headed I feel drafting the stipulations. After all, I put off writing my first will until I was fifty, unwilling to face the possibility that I might not be around forever. My ex had to terrify me with grim visions of our children impoverished by probate court before I'd acknowledge death in black and white. Now here I am taking the measure of my death like a cord of firewood I need to get in before the first snow.

I enjoy making these plans. I imagine the will operating as a supernatural machine devised to carry out my plans after I'm gone. It's comforting to know that the world can be controlled from beyond the grave. A trickier scheme is required to send messages while you're alive, but unable to communicate. The Lawyer asks how I'd want to be treated if I were on a life-support system with little hope of recovery, and unable to express myself.

"Pull the plug."

"Okay, we'll draft a living will. Basically you don't want any heroic measures taken to keep you alive under those circumstances."

I nod.

"But what if they pull the plug and you don't die?" he asks.

"Like a coma? And I'm lying there in a veggie state?"

"Some people go on like that for years."

"No chance of getting laid again?"

He laughs.

"Shoot me," I say.

"That's illegal in a hospital."

"I thought dying was scary, now you're really giving me nightmares."

"There is a way out," he says. "Designate someone, your next of kin usually, durable power of attorney. If, God forbid, you get in a situation like that, you stipulate that under those circumstances you want food and water withheld."

I nod.

"But keep up the painkillers?" he suggests.

"Glad you mentioned it."

The Lawyer adds that he thinks I should specify my beneficiaries by name. "Instead of saying you want to divide your estate equally between your children, you name the kids."

"I assume you have a reason."

"Some old girlfriend might come out of the woods and say, Thirty years ago I slept with this guy and I never told him but there's this kid . . ."

"I don't think so."

"That's what Jefferson's ancestors said until DNA testing came along and proved different. They can tell now."

"Whatever happened to *Rest in Peace*?"

"There's no money in it."

"Sounds like a good argument for cremation. I have a deep fear of being exhumed."

The Lawyer tells me he'll draft the will, living will, and power of attorney, and I can come back in a few days and sign it.

"What about the funeral?" I ask. The Lawyer spins around in his black leather recliner and looks out the window. The first snow of the year is melting off the roof. There will be more.

"I don't like to think about funerals," he says. "It's depressing." He lights another Winston. I wonder if second-hand smoke is healthier, without the additives. "People are funny about funerals," he says, filling the room with heavenly blue clouds. "My mother refuses to be buried next to my father. Why? Because he's buried next to his mother, and they never got along. But the old lady's been dead thirty years!"

"What about you?"

"There's a veteran's cemetery on a hill in town. Veterans get a stone, and I'll put my rank on it."

"I was wondering if it's a good idea to pay a funeral home ahead of time?"

"If you've got your plans set, sure. The money goes into an escrow account until it's needed. The funeral home earns interest, but your price doesn't go up."

"What if I drop dead in Iceland?"

"Nothing's foolproof."

No wonder so many people prefer cremation. It wipes out all the uncertainty about post-mortem procedures. Tell your next of kin you want to be incinerated, and you can die just about anywhere and have your wish come true. Forget prepayments, surprise embalming, and air trays. Forget the coffin for that matter. If you're dead-set on a headstone, have the ashes buried under it.

"Just make sure you tell your plans to your next of kin, or whomever you designate," the Lawyer continues. "I've seen families get into terrible fights with their church pastor over whether the casket should be open or closed. They fight over the words on the headstone—*father, husband,* whatever. The same goes for personal property. Make a list of your valuables, specify who gets what, and give it to your next of kin or executor. It doesn't hurt to add that if they don't like your decisions, they get nothing. Otherwise it can be crazy. I've seen families get into fistfights over an old christening dress. They brawl, they cry, they make up. The parents must be tossing and turning in their graves."

The Lawyer says that according to traditional Jewish and Roman Catholic law, survivors are obliged to visit a gravesite one year after death, then their obligations to the deceased were complete. A couple of pastors I spoke to later had never heard of the custom. Asking around, I did find out the roots of Memorial Day, which we're patriotically told is a commemoration of American war dead. Actually, it's a holiday with ancient pagan origins, set aside annually for the tidying up of burial grounds. Imagine the whole country flocking to the cemeteries on May 30th, straightening gravestones and planting daisies, honoring everyone from ancestors to unknowns. Unlike the Mexican Day of the Dead, set in darkening November, Memorial Day falls at the start of summer. A day to acknowledge death and simultaneously celebrate the renewal of life. Now that's a ritual worth reviving.

The Lawyer looks at his watch and guesses that his manacled client must be pretty upset by now. It's time to go. The sunlight dazzles when I step out the door, and I feel pleasantly lightheaded. Plans have been made, issues addressed, the immortality machine primed and ready. For the first time in my life, the judicial system makes me smile.

THE ASTROLOGER opens the door and raises her hand against the morning sunlight.

"Wow!" she says.

What else can you say when it's December in Vermont and as the days shorten, they're also getting unnaturally warmer? The November snow has dribbled away, and the ponds and lakes are a month late icing over. We set up a couple of chairs and a table on the emerald lawn. The Astrologer lays out a chart she's made for me. It's covered with arcane planetary symbols, signs of the Zodiac, angles and houses. I have no idea what any of it means, but that doesn't prevent me from enjoying this weird warmth and her undiluted attention to my unique destiny. Is this what it feels like to live in L.A.?

The Astrologer points out that my sun is in Gemini, and I nod. Until today that was the scope of my astrological knowledge. Over the years I've checked out the newspapers occasionally, amused when the horoscopes seem accurate, more amused when they're wrong. Nevertheless, there does seem to be some accuracy to the tabloid diagnosis of Gemini souls—divided, tortured—and it's been some consolation to know that Bob Dylan and the Marquis de Sade are also members of this "suffering" tribe. It's this dark side I'm here to explore, in order to find an explanation for my recent preoccupation with death.

The Astrologer's reading bears little resemblance to my self-image as a fortune-cookie Gemini. Apparently there's more to astral divination than the sun's position at birth. There's also the rising sign, moon, planets, houses, and their relationship to each other and the signs of the zodiac. My chart is arrayed with more than four dozen icons, triangles, glyphs, and numbers, an alien code I'm trusting the Astrologer to break.

I've known the Astrologer since she starred in a video I produced a few years ago. It was an oddball story about a backwoods biker-woman charming a logger out of a cord of firewood by spinning a tale about alien UFOs, and her quirky con job was the highlight of the film. She's worked as an actress, theatrical director, psychotherapist, hypnotherapist, and her latest manifestation, astrologer. I called her after I met someone at a party, an amateur astrologer, who hinted that there's a dark side to astrology that no one discusses. My antennae went up. He led me off to a corner where we wouldn't be overheard.

"I've been doing research," he whispered, warily scanning the room. "There's a lot of stuff astrologers don't talk about. They won't touch it."

I told him not to worry. Nobody wants to talk about death. Why should astrologers be any different?

"But that's the point. It used to be a big deal, a whole dimension of astrology."

Before he had a chance to say anything more, his wife found him and grabbed his elbow like a truant schoolkid and hauled him away.

A couple of weeks later I phoned another astrologer who gave me a runaround when I brought up the Reaper, as if I had a plague he didn't want to catch.

That's when I remembered the actress-therapist-star gazer, and called to tell her I was interested in having my chart done. We made a date, and before she hung up, I mentioned the D word. I'd been worrying about it. She asked how old I was. I told her.

"Sounds natural," she said.

SITTING IN THE warm sun now, paying serious money to have my horoscope charted, it feels like a long way from chainsaws and sugar-on-snow. Indeed, the Astrologer tells me, the world frequency is changing, big-time.

"Like this freaky weather?"

"That could be part of it." She's wearing a black baseball cap and sunglasses—no turquoise, no crystals—more like a beat poet than a New Age fortune-teller. She tells me that her astrology is "soul based," meaning it's her hunch that we come into this world with a blueprint we asked for, that we choose a life purposely to work certain things out. It sounds similar to what Buddhists say about karma and rebirth, how we move from one life to the next, evolving up or down the karmic wheel until we decide to get off. In other words, when you look in the mirror remind yourself, You Asked For It.

Lately, she tells me, she's heard from several past-life channelers that the layover time of souls in transition has been speeding up. It used to be that a soul had about one hundred and twenty years between incarnations, before saying, "I'll take those parents down there!" Now the delay is down to zero, and souls are coming back as fast as they leave. "There are as many souls down here now as ever existed in history, plus new ones."

"Where do the new ones come from then?"

"Where does anyone come from? That's the big question."

"Why would they all want to come back so quickly now?"

"Because we're seeming to need to transform the planet in some way, we're changing the vibration, the frequency on the planet, for some larger purpose. Not just for us, not just to survive on the Earth, but it's literally this huge time, and most people don't feel the universe is going to end. They feel all the doomsday prophecies have now passed, we've gotten past them on some level."

Hopeful as that sounds, I have to tell her I've been having some doomsday fears of my own, and I'm not sure they've passed. I wonder if they might be connected to my "blueprint." She says that many elements of the chart do mirror my character, my work, and the darkness I've been facing. Scorpio rising fits my tendency to dig down deep into obsessional projects and not let go. Coffins, anyone? Moon in Pisces suggests a hankering for art, drugs, and alcohol. Who me, officer? The Pisces moon, with Venus and Jupiter in Cancer, indicates a strong affinity for water, borne out in a career designing ponds and writing about aquaculture.

"And death?"

The Astrologer shakes her head. If I want someone to predict my time of death, I have to look somewhere else. Her approach to astrology is more "positive," using people's charts to identify their personality characteristics, and to help them map their own way. But she admits that there is another school of astrology, the Eastern Hindu branch, which is concerned with death. Remember the Egyptians, she says, who inherited astrological techniques from Babylon and built a culture focused exclusively on preparations for death and the afterlife. In fact my chart is riddled with dark forces. Gemini may be associated with humor, but in the Tarot deck it's also the thirteenth death card.

"Death as the cosmic joke." She grins.

Gemini is also characterized as a very *puer* sign. As Dylan sang, "May you stay forever young." That can mean big trouble in the face of the aging process.

"No wonder death seems so freaky to you," she says. She tells me that because Saturn had been in my sixth house recently, I could expect to feel rundown and depleted, and then there was Pluto, the "bulldozer of the universe," which she says had been boring down hard. Apparently I've been going through a Pluto "transit" for the past couple of years, and not only had Pluto been strengthening the "puer" resistance to aging, but it had been in opposition to my sun sign, with a huge potential for fatality.

"A Pluto transit is hell on earth," she says, adding that because this planet is so distant and moves slowly in relation to the rest of the planets, it's like a razor blade grinding back and forth over an old wound. On top of that, Pluto had been in a "trine" to my natal Pluto. "It's a once in a lifetime kind of period," she says. "You go through fire and it seems like you won't survive. It takes you down into the underworld."

She says that the Pluto transit had been going on for the past two years, which coincides with my divorce, depression, heart palpitations, a book deal that fell through, and a nasty problem with woodchucks in my garden.

"It's lucky you survived," she says, explaining that Pluto transits are the most common reason people come to her. "I see it all the time. The world doesn't make sense any longer, you can't get a grip. It's a phenomenal thing, you can't control a Pluto transit. It levels the ground."

I wonder if she would have revealed all this if I'd come to see her two years ago, and I think I understand why she doesn't make death predictions. A lot of people might prefer to blow their brains out before getting run over by the bulldozer of the universe.

The Astrologer tells me that with Pluto now out of opposition, and Saturn moving out of my sixth house, it's time to heal. "Now you need to recover! You need to rest!" How come doctors never talk to you like this?

"You're in a rebirth phase," she says soothingly, explaining that while Pluto levels the earth, it can also be considered a builder, laying the groundwork for new growth. "There's a nodal return coming up. Conceivably you'll be able to use it creatively and allow a deep transition of self. You can mine it for something."

She tells me that the best thing I can do is to conjure up some future state of happiness, even if I do it just a few minutes a day, and gradually I'll find myself in that very place. It's the healer talking now, the cognitive therapist, the Dale Carnegie positive thinker, and I remember a time not long ago when the cynic in me would have sneered. But my life is at stake now, and besides, what can I lose? I just read an article in *The New York Times* about placebos being more effective than pills. But how does building my coffin fit into the picture? Is it really an antidote to depression, or just a morbid bath in a psychic buffalo wallow?

The Astrologer goes into the house and returns with a book. "This guy is a very good astrologer," she says. "It's not exactly my cup of tea, but you might find it interesting." She hands me the book. *The Astrology of Death.* "He's a fun writer," she assures me, but the book feels heavy in my hand.

THE ASTROLOGY OF DEATH is a self-published guide by Richard Houck, an astrologer who's done consulting work for investors and blue-chip corporations, but couldn't find a publisher for a book about predicting death. (Not as traumatic as the situation of Nostradamus, who had to flee France because of his astrological predictions, which are still coming true four hundred years later.) Conventional marketing wisdom has it that the astrology crowd isn't interested in death, although Houck points out that Hindu astrologers have used predictive techniques for centuries, forecasting death and prescribing gemstones, chants, and rituals to forestall it.

Houck's book is filled with charts of famous and unknown dead, which he claims can be read to demonstrate that their check-out times were fated. John Lennon, for instance, was destined to world fame and a shocking death by a combination of lunar eclipses before and after his birth, a malign Pluto, and an unfortunate Saturn. Charts for Elvis, Richard Nixon, John F. Kennedy, Abraham Lincoln, and many others are accompanied by narratives explaining the celestial logic of their deaths. Looking over these charts and reading the occult explanations, I realize I have no basis for evaluating Houck's technique, and don't want to learn. The idea of knowing the time of my death seems appalling.

Yet Houck makes a compelling argument for this taboo art, reminding us that confronting a fear can often loosen its grip, and that if we all knew when we were going to die our lives might be spiritually enhanced. On a more practical level, he alerts us to the financial advantage of delaying life insurance payments until near the end. He also claims that a more direct approach to death is in the stars, particularly since Pluto moved into Scorpio in 1993, which he links to our *fin de siècle* interest in reincarnation, hospices, death psychology, physician-assisted euthanasia, and suicide. In fact, as modern medicine blurs the line between life and death, and people struggle with ethical dilemmas over the use of life-extending technology, he suggests an astrology chart might be more useful than a doctor's chart to answer the more important question: when am I *supposed* to die.

Yet I'm puzzled to read that Houck recommends astrologers refrain from making death predictions. What's the point of writing a book about a skill you feel shouldn't be used? If he wants to defang death, why the cop-out? I call Houck at his Maryland office to find out. He begins by telling me why he wrote the book.

"My objective was to catch the eye of Western astrologers, to show them that Eastern astrology has a stronger foundation." He says that when he first developed an interest in astrology he used conventional Western systems, only to become annoyed with their methods and results. He especially objected to the "prissy attitude" Western astrologers have about death. Indeed, his book is full of sly humor and unflattering references to astrology's New Age platitudes.

He was also aware that the majority of his readers would be professional astrologers in a powerful position to influence their clients. "I was concerned about people who might have had a recent illness, or experienced the death of a relative, or might be thinking about suicide. I knew that a death date could go into peoples' heads and create a negative fear effect. As for the astrologer, your life will get morbid if you get into death predictions. It's not a constructive use of astrology. You also have to be careful how you interpret death. It might not be a literal death, it can be the death of a relative, or a divorce, which can be just as damaging."

Houck also had a more personal reason for writing the book. "I was going through a bad patch," he admits, "and the book fit my mood. In fact, writing it was obnoxious. But I have a theory that when you're down in a ditch, it's important to keep working and when you come out of it, you'll have something in your hand."

Indeed, Houck did cycle back up, and four years after its publication, *The Astrology of Death* is scheduled to be translated into French, German, and Portuguese. "It's got a dedicated audience," he says, adding that he gets responses daily to the book, abuse as well as praise from both astrology camps, East and West.

As for his own death, Houck did the calculations, and published his chart at the end of the book. As he interprets it, he's got plenty of time. "But then again," he concedes, "we're all potentially wrong. I really don't care."

As we talk, I get the impression of someone at peace with himself and his fate. As he points out, astrology, and death itself, are part of a cosmic plan light years beyond Jerry Falwell and his moral majority. Until we develop a new foundation for mental peace, people will be looking for relief in all the wrong places.

I still I don't want to know when I'm going to die. But it's comforting to think that if the day has already been determined, there's not a thing I can do about it.

THE ANATOMIST has generously invited me to his house, in spite of a frantic schedule. It's a couple of days before Christmas, he spent the morning coralling a bull for shipment to the slaughterhouse, and he's recovering from a full-tilt teaching schedule at the nearby medical school. He stands barefoot on the front steps, tosses the wandering chickens a handful of corn, and invites me in.

I'm here because the news is full of bewildering stories about organ donations and transplants, and I feel vaguely guilty that I haven't made plans to give my body to medical science after I croak. The blank organ donor box on my driver's license nags at me, another unresolved funeral issue I've been happy to ignore. The truth is, some of these "anatomical gift" stories are so bizarre, my gut feeling is to decline. I heard about one guy who wanted to donate a kidney to his daughter. The problem is that he's in prison, he has only one kidney, and if he does make the donation he'll be on dialysis for the rest of his life, at taxpayers' expense. Then there's the heart transplant recipient who had a complete personality switch after the operation. I can't help imagining Frankenstein rising off the O.R. table when I hear this.

Compared to transplants, cadaver donations seem downright old-fashioned, so I figure I'll start off with the basics. The Anatomist offers me a cup of tea and a chocolate biscotti, and we sit down to discuss the medical school's body-donation program, which he runs. From somewhere upstairs a recording of the Grateful Dead fills the house with Jerry

Garcia's immortal guitar licks. The Anatomist explains that he needs thirty-five new bodies a year to fill the teaching requirements of the dissecting lab. He hands me a flyer detailing the program, which appears to involve little more than filling out a donor card. He adds that he usually has more bodies than he needs. No advertising, no public relations, all by word of mouth.

"Isn't that amazing, people donating their bodies out of the blue?"

"They just assume that medical schools take bodies," he shrugs, "and a lot of societies fighting the funeral industry write us up. Donation is a way to save funeral costs, although in my experience mostly the aim of it is altruistic. In fact, some families combine it with financial gifts."

"And if I want to donate my body?"

"You fill out a card, discuss it with your next of kin. But there's an interesting legal point. The simple fact is that you have no say in the disposition of your remains. Nobody does. When you're dead you can't do anything. You can't will your body anywhere. You can't decide whether you want to be cremated or buried at sea or anything else. It's not your decision. Your body is not part of your estate. You can leave your land and your car and your this and that to anybody you wish, but you can't leave your body. The decision is the prerogative of the next of kin. It's kind of an interesting concept that you don't have any control over your body when you're dead."

I'm tempted to remind the Anatomist that often we don't seem to have much control over our bodies when we're alive, and life and death have more in common than might appear.

"It goes back to ancient common law in Europe and England," he continues. "I guess it was sort of a biblical interpretation, dust to dust; once you had died, you weren't property, you were back to dust. And actually in medical training there was a time when dissecting was legal but there was no way to get bodies. In other words the King or the Pope would say, There's nothing wrong with dissection, it's not immoral or anything, so go ahead and dissect! So you say, Great, but where do I get a body from?"

The Anatomist looks at me for an answer and I recall the Graveyard Guide's history of the town cemetery, and the light on the little girl's grave.

"The source was grave robbing! Common law held that you couldn't be convicted of grave robbing, it wasn't a crime, because a body isn't anything, it's just dirt once it's dead. Actually throughout history many families to thwart the grave robbers would take a piece of real property and put it in the corpse. For example, if I was burying you I could take a little piece of handkerchief and stick it under your tongue or put something in your ear. A piece of property! And then if somebody stole your body, okay, we could hang them for stealing the piece of cloth. Out of that tradition we've evolved a situation where the body isn't property and its disposition goes to the next of kin. The bottom line is, you cannot donate your body to the medical school. What you do is fill out a form indicating your wishes and you have your family witness it. And if the family objects we won't take the body. No matter what you might have said."

So it's not just funerals that are for the living, but decisions about anatomical gifts, too. The living get all the breaks.

"I once had a case where somebody said, Well, I know my husband wanted to be there, but I don't. And I said, You're right! He ain't going! Likewise, suppose you decided for whatever reason you did not want to be a body donor, you thought it was wrong. You could tattoo on your forehead, NOT A BODY DONOR, and whenever you die, whoever your next of kin is, they can call me up and say, 'This guy passed away, I don't want to pay for a funeral. Will you take the body?' And if I say yes, that's the end of the line. They're the next of kin, they're saying I can have that body. Your wishes are totally irrelevant. Now that's never happened, and in fact we will not accept under any circumstances somebody who has not specifically while they're alive said that's what they want to do by filling out our forms. I get calls all the time, Oh, somebody just died and they always wanted to be a body donor but he never filled out the forms, and I say, Well, he should have. I won't take him."

No pussyfooting around here, none of the sugar coating I'd run into with the Undertaker. And yet what the Anatomist says next impresses me because it seems to override the clinical detachment essential to building a career on dead bodies.

"One of the things that's important to us is that I can tell the med students that everyone down there wanted to be, that these are people who said, I want these med students to learn on me. And that changes the students' attitudes. They're not sitting there saying, Gee, is this some executed prisoner or some unclaimed body? Or what did this person ever do wrong to end up in the lab? So the students treat these people as if they're people. *Patients.* I want to be able to look the students in the eye and tell them that every person down there went out of their way, came to me and said, Hey, I want to fill out the forms, this is what I want, this is what I want done with my body, I want to help medical students and education."

And what about me? Do I want to help medical students and education? What about my debt to medicine? No doubt, I've benefited from cadaver studies, and so have my kids. Do I owe it to society to sacrifice my carcass for the greater good? No way! The thought of having my body chopped and diced gives me the creeps. Not even the thought of saving funeral costs, money my kids could no doubt put to better use, offsets the shivers this grisly business gives me.

"You want to see the gross lab?"

"What?"

"The gross anatomy lab, would you like to see it?" The Anatomist explains that while the med students are away on winter break, the lab can be opened to visitors. Otherwise, during the semester, with body parts all over the tables and students slicing away, the lab is off limits.

Christmas in the morgue. Lucky me.

A COUPLE OF DAYS later we meet in the basement of the medical school. The hallways are empty, and in the faculty lounge a Christmas tree blinks mutely in the corner while the Anatomist thumbs through a newspaper. This must be the most peaceful place in the whole holiday-crazed valley, but instead of feeling tranquil, I'm wired.

"Ready for the grand tour?" he asks, folding up the paper.

I follow him into the hall and down the stairs. First stop, the morgue. Beside the door, there's a laminated color poster of the human anatomy, with bold letters across the bottom. XANAX. Why is it that everywhere I go in the medical establishment I find calendars and notepads and ballpoint pens sponsored by Zoloff, Paxil, Wellbutrin, Xanax, and Prozac?

The morgue is small and cold, about the size of a bus-station bathroom and just as friendly. There's a blue, plastic body bag on a stainless-steel table in the middle of the room, and it's not empty. Through the open zipper at the top, I catch a glimpse of something gray, like clay, and I realize that it's someone's face.

"This is where we prepare the bodies," the Anatomist says. He points out an empty drip bottle hanging from the ceiling, which I assume was recently connected to the body on the table. He explains that once a body is embalmed it remains here in cold storage for eight months. "For safety reasons," he says, "because we don't know what viruses and things are in a body. Our embalming solution is not a cosmetic solution like funeral directors use. We're trying to preserve and sterilize the tissues, so we use some dangerous chemicals, basically. The body is not very lifelike when we're done, it's sort of gray and stiff. And then once the eight months are up, we can actually use it. When I pull a body out for the med students to use, it's out for six months."

This isn't a place to linger, not if you've got a choice, and I follow the Anatomist out the door, around the corner, and into the dissecting lab. It's warm in here, which is an improvement, but there's a sour smell that reminds me of the funeral home basement. It's a much larger room filled with more stainless-steel tables, each with a blue-bagged body on top. The door closes behind us and the Anatomist and I are alone in the silent room. It's an eerie sight, twenty-five bodies resting between semesters like campers in mummy bags waiting for the rising bell. A door at the far end of the room opens and a man wheels a silver tank of liquid nitrogen through the room and out the other door without saying a word.

The Anatomist explains that the dissecting process starts with work on the back and upper limbs, and then moves to thorax, abdomen, lower limbs, pelvis, neck, shoulders, and brain. "The whole works," he says proudly. He points out the body tags attached to each bag, explaining that there are strict rules against moving body parts from one table to another for comparative purposes, unless they are tagged by an instructor. "We're very careful that each part gets back where it belongs because we do our own cremations, and we have to make sure we don't mix up the bodies."

After six months of dissection, the remains are cremated at the medical school, and the next of kin then have a choice. "We can bury the ashes at our cost at the medical school," he explains, "or send the ashes to the family or a funeral director or a cemetery of their choosing." Except for the obituary, the medical school handles everything from the death certificate and body pickup to disposal. Considering that the average cost of a funeral today is five thousand dollars, it's a significant savings.

I walk around the room, past the dissecting instruments and tissue pails, and wonder what it's like when the students are here.

"Busy," the Anatomist tells me. "And it's not always students." He tells me about a recent visit from a surgeon who wanted to do a transplant and used a cadaver to practice on. The operation was a success, and the patient went home with his big toe for a thumb.

I think about the people in this basement who helped that transplant succeed, who were helping a new generation of doctors, and I had to admire them. What does it take to volunteer for the gross anatomy lab? Courage? Faith in science? A healthy indifference to dismemberment probably helps. Whatever it is, I've seen enough. Somehow I can't imagine myself in one of those blue bags. Just not hero material, I guess.

Leaving the medical school, I step outside and take a gulp of cold air. I feel shaken by what I've seen. Not only the lifeless gray face and the patches of tissue and hair in the stainless-steel pails, but the blunt finality of death. I can't help feeling that life is rushing by way too fast and I'm squandering it.

I T'S HELPFUL to know that you can beat the cost of a funeral by donating your cadaver to science, but your opportunity to be a dead hero doesn't end there. Check off the organ donor box on your driver's license, and you can be eligible to recycle your living heart, lungs, kidneys, eyes, pancreas, liver, even your skin. The critical issue is to be in good condition—brain dead but otherwise shipshape—and confident your next of kin will execute your wishes. Most organ donors qualify because of car smashups, which accounts for the conveniently marked driver's license. Testament to the power of modern technology to redeem its bloodiest excesses. Actually, this practice of finding a silver lining in the clouds of carnage began on the battlefields of Belgium, where the British defeated Napoleon in 1816. Included among the victors' spoils were the teeth of dead soldiers, which dentists in London later fashioned into dentures popularly known as Waterloo teeth.

Donating vital organs to save a life may seem more valuable than supplying a cadaver, but it won't get you a free funeral. The medical establishment has to be careful that it's not accused of encouraging survivors to pull the plug for financial gain. Who really knows when someone is brain dead with no chance for recovery? The newspapers occasionally surprise us with tales of comatose patients waking up after months of unconsciousness. The Astrologer tells me she has a theory that pulling the plug on comatose patients screws up their karma. Despite being unconscious, she feels that they're busily working out their fate while lying there inert.

There were 19,998 transplants in the United States in 1997, but three times that number of patients were unable to find a donor. Medical advances will only increase the demand for organ donors. Where will these donations come from? Do we all have a moral obligation to consign our organs to donor banks in case of "brain death"? Would you want a transplant if it might save your life, and if so, wouldn't you be morally obliged to sign up as a donor yourself? These are complex questions involving practical and spiritual dilemmas. Who gets the organs that are available? The sickest, the richest, the most likely to recover? What about drug addicts, alcoholics, and smokers—should they receive organ donations? What role does religion play in all this? Christian Scientists and Jehovah's Witnesses are prohibited from accepting transplants. Should their children also be excluded? On the other hand, Pope John Paul II has recommended organ donation, comparing it to Christ's sacrifice. Are Roman Catholics obliged to sign up as organ donors?

Many Native Americans believe that a dead person's body must be returned to nature in order for the soul to pass on to the next world. Otherwise, the spirit is condemned to stalk the earth as a restless ghost (unless having an organ transferred to another person is a way of returning it to nature?). Hence, their objection to museums that hold onto Indian skeletons and other remains. Superstitious nonsense? Who can say that widespread transplanting won't have an aberrant effect on the invisible, supernatural cosmos? Many spiritual teachers believe that the heart is the soul.

There's also the question of who gets a second chance. With forty-four percent of the country unable to afford basic health insurance, the answer seems obvious. What are the ethical implications of putting the heart of a poor young black man killed by a drive-by shooter into the chest of a cigar-smoking WASP who had a heart attack on the floor of the stock exchange? Does it matter? Where is the quest for immortality taking us?

Perhaps most fascinating are the psychological and spiritual unknowns of organ transplants. The father of one donor became obsessed with following his dead son's heart around. A kidney recipient was oppressed with guilt, a bizarre new twist in survivor's syndrome. A staff member of the New England Organ Donor Bank told me that because of such potentially emotional reactions, organ banks usually require donors and recipients to remain unknown to each other.

Noble as these medical advances seem, I can't help feeling that there's something twisted going on. The increasing potential to cheat death makes the ultimate certainty harder to accept, so we repress and drug ourselves, and in the process lose our appreciation for life itself. Indeed, what about life? The planet is crowded and polluted, but instead of dealing with those problems, everybody's zonked out watching videos and surfing the net. Are we turning into high-tech vampires living vicarious lives, and ever longer ones at that? But hey, aren't vampires supposed to live forever?

THE SCREENWRITER lives alone in a rambling old colonial a mile south of the local college. The driveway is boilerplate ice following another aborted snowstorm, the third icing we've had in as many weeks, and after lurching from the car to the front door, I take a deep breath. Nothing like a sheet of ice to stir up speculations about the brittleness of the bones.

The Screenwriter invites me in, puts some coffee in the microwave, and lights a cigarette, moving around the room as uncertainly as I crossed the ice. The Screenwriter is blind. Deteriorating retinas, he explains, no cure for it. Over the past few years he's had to give up first his teaching position in the film studies program at the college, then reading, and finally television. Three shopping bags full of unopened videos sit on the floor in the dining room, a gold mine of new movies sent by the Academy of Motion Picture Arts and Sciences, but of course he won't be able to cast his Oscar votes. Getting old is no picnic, but the irony here seems especially cruel.

We sit down at the kitchen table. Between us is a pencil sharpener. THE OLD GRIND it says. I imagine a mountain of pencil stubs piled up after fifty years of screenplays, beginning with *The Red Ball Express,* a World War II picture for Universal in 1951. His screenplays for *Peyton Place* and *Rear Window* won Academy Award nominations. His most recent work was the script for *Iron Will,* released by Disney in 1994. But the stories for which he's known best are those he did with Alfred

Hitchcock: *Rear Window, The Man Who Knew Too Much, To Catch a Thief,* and the quirky, underrated *The Trouble With Harry,* one of my top-ten desert island pictures.

The Trouble With Harry is an offbeat yarn about a dead body discovered in a Vermont pasture, and the succession of village eccentrics who get tangled up in a screwball burial scheme. The cast includes Shirley MacLaine in her film debut, Mildred Dunnock, and John Forsythe, with a splendid score by Bernard Hermann, the first of his many successful collaborations with Hitchcock. Watching MacLaine's turn as a kooky single mom chattering cheerfully to the corpse of her brother-in-law, I feel as if I'm witnessing the birth of the New Age as the impressionable young actress buys whole heartedly into the script, anticipating her evolution into the best-selling guru of Woo-Woo Supernaturality. The Screenwriter deserves another award: Father of the Age of Harry.

The story begins when Edmund Gwenn, as a retired old sea captain, discovers the corpse while out hunting rabbits. Certain that his own stray shot was responsible, and terrified of what the police will do if he reports the death, he plans a cover-up. More locals stumble onto the scene, and a bizarre homemade funeral develops as the conspirators trade opinions on the requirements for a proper resting spot.

> "A place with a certain character and attractiveness . . ."
> ". . . facing west so Harry can watch the setting sun."
> "Cozy in winter . . ."
> ". . . cool in summer."
> "You know, I'm half envying Harry . . ."
> "It wouldn't take much longer to dig it twice as wide."

Keeping Harry underground turns out to be every bit as complicated as deciphering various motivations for killing him, and the tale spins out into an affectionate send-up of puritan New England, formula mysteries, sex, and death. Set against a backdrop of golden fall foliage and a nostalgic New England village, with the elderly Gwenn courting Mildred Natwick's late-blooming spinster, the film has a dotty, elegiac quality, as if it were shot on a backlot in paradise. One of Hitchcock's biographers, Donald Spoto, suggests that for the director, *Harry* is "a denial of death and burial." I occasionally rerun the film for pretty much the same reason. It's a soothing tonic against bouts of dread, shot in my own backyard.

In 1955, the same year *The Trouble With Harry* was released, Hitchcock began his legendary television series, *Alfred Hitchcock Presents.* Television enabled Hitchcock to bring his fascinations into American living rooms. I'll never forget those droll opening monologues, as Hitchcock stepped into his own jowly silhouette, accompanied by Gonoud's "Funeral March of the Marionettes," and then turned to the audience. He might muse on the efficiency of a medieval torture rack, or lie across railroad tracks, explaining that there were some things an airplane just couldn't do. This wasn't Boris Karloff or Dracula, it was an overweight Englishman whose delight in the macabre was contagious, film director as funeral director. It was the perfect antidote to that rival ringmaster of 1950s TV, Walt Disney. In an era when few people dared say the word, Hitchcock domesticated *death.*

When I learned that the Screenwriter lived only a few miles south of me, I called, hoping for a chance to ask what it was that made Hitchcock tick, and Harry, too. There's more to all this than funeral homes and coffins, and I wondered if the Screenwriter might have some insights into the American perception of death. Did working with Hitchcock have any influence on his own attitude to mortality?

"When I worked on *The Trouble With Harry,* Harry wasn't real to me," the Screenwriter begins. "He was sort of a statue or something, but the lives of the people who surrounded him were real to me. So that's how we wrote the picture. None of the people who observed him, dug him up, buried him, whatever, were concerned with the inevitability of their own lives. They were just trying to live as well as they could. And Harry didn't teach them that lesson—that there was a time when you were going to be lying in a field. They never thought of that, or at least I don't think they did."

"Hitch had wanted to do it for a long time," the Screenwriter goes on, explaining the origins of *The Trouble With Harry*, which was based on a British novel by John Trevor Story. "But Paramount didn't see it as a profitable picture. But Hitch decided that after *Rear Window,* and *To Catch a Thief,* and *The Man Who Knew Too Much,* they owed him something." The Screenwriter laughs. "They owed him the privilege of doing this movie. When it first came out it didn't make a lot of money in America, but it was very big in Europe."

I recall my conversations with the Undertaker and the Stone Carver concerning how differently Europeans react to death. I imagine a long line for Harry in Paris, all the way past an *haute couture* coffin shop.

"At some theatres it stayed for a year. And then it came back to America and people saw in it more virtue than they had the first time, because the first time they expected a traditional Hitchcock picture, which they didn't get. But he was delighted with it, and we had a wonderful time making it."

Although a man who was notoriously tight-fisted with money, Hitchcock undertook the project well aware of its financial liabilities. It was short on suspense and long on the kind of amiably wacky humor relished in England. He would always consider it one of his favorite films. In fact, when Hitchcock hired a writer for the television monologues, he screened *The Trouble With Harry* as a prototype for the deadpan humor he was after. Oddly enough, the director failed to make one of his trademark cameos in the film. Or perhaps he figured Harry was a good stand-in.

I wonder what Hitchcock would have made of Ginseng Willard and his funeral preparations. Perhaps he'd open with a comic shot of Ginseng trying to take his own measurements, then a close-up of him hard at work, sawing, hammering, and sanding. When the homemade coffin is finished, would we see him tempted to get in for a test run? Lying down, he smiles with satisfaction. Will he find a worm in the wood? Naturally he'll want to make sure the lid fits, so he pulls it down tight. So far, so good. But wait, it's stuck! THE END. *Moral:* Preneed arrangements are commendable only up to a point.

I ask the Screenwriter if he thinks Hitchcock was working out a fear of death in his films, *Harry* especially. After all, it's the story of a guy who won't stay buried, and the main characters spend most of the time with shovels in their hands, burying and exhuming him again and again.

"Hitch had a fear, a wonderment about death," the Screenwriter acknowledges. "In his later days at Universal when he was making *Family Plot,* he used to come into the office every morning and say to the secretary, Do you think this will be the day? And he began to drink wine and brandy, it was a mixture, to anesthetize him against what he thought was the inevitable."

In *The Trouble With Harry,* Hitchcock was able to make laughter from his dread, as any of us might do on those good days when we convince ourselves that death is natural, acceptable, "inevitable." But the good days don't last. Following *The Trouble With Harry,* Hitchcock's films grew darker and more grotesque, eventually "crossing the border line into blood," as the Screenwriter puts it disdainfully, "with *Psycho.*"

Perhaps, I speculate, he was trying to probe deeper.

"Yes," the Screenwriter nods, "into the market."

After *The Trouble With Harry,* the Screenwriter and Hitchcock had a falling out. Hitchcock didn't like the recognition his writer was getting for his contributions to the films, and they never worked together again. The Screenwriter continued to work in Hollywood, then eventually returned gratefully to his native New England. A few years ago his wife died, and he deeply misses her. With fifty years of radio scripts and screenplays to his credit, he will be remembered for a deft blending of comedy and suspense, the trademark Hitchcock style. But where, in fact, does a lifetime of writing about life's demons leave you?

"You know, I was sitting here this morning thinking about my birthday coming up in May, when I'll be eighty, and my children are going to come and visit me and everything, and I think to myself, Do they suspect something I don't know? Eighty is the time when you start thinking . . . my profession is gone, my teaching is gone, I'm sitting here unable to see, and I don't know what I'm sitting here for. I have always had something to look forward to, and that's the problem with old age, you don't have anything to look forward to, except the possibility of death. I don't have an Academy Award to look forward to, another big picture to look forward to . . ." And then he laughs. "I don't dwell on it really. I know it's there and I have to do the best I can to get by through the day. Some days it's more difficult than others.

"Death doesn't frighten me or worry me or anything. It will happen as everything happens in life. I don't think about it."

The Screenwriter isn't fishing for sympathy. He's a stubborn old New Englander, proud to be here. "People say, What are you doing, alone in this huge house? Why don't you get an apartment in California or something? And I say, I don't want to be any other place. I wouldn't go to New York. My children want me to go to Atlanta or Houston or Los Angeles. No way. I'm a New Englander, even though I hate the ice that's outside." He laughs and lights a cigarette. "I was brought up in New Hampshire and then Maine and I have a different look at things, I respond to things differently. *The Trouble With Harry* reflected my feeling about New England. It's not only a refuge, but it's a lovely way to live."

I'm struck by the eerie similarity between the Screenwriter's predicament and the character he created for *Rear Window,* a crippled Jimmy Stewart trapped in his apartment. Life mimicking fiction? Fate tempted once too often? The Screenwriter morphing into Stephen King? Now there's a story, but instead of pitching it, I'm more curious about his thoughts on the redeeming qualities of art—books, film, sculpture. Do they take the sting out of death?

"A friend of mine wrote children's books, one of them about my son. She's gone now. And she said, The people will remember me, and remember this for years to come. I think it's a large factor in creativity and the writing of books and so forth. To leave your stamp on the world. I don't know if it's comforting when you die, but at least you know you're not going to be forgotten. That's of course why the Romans and the Greeks built all those statues and everything, so that even though life is transitory, they would never be forgotten. I think it's true. In that respect I felt sorry for Harry because he had no meaning." The Screenwriter laughs. "He didn't contribute to anybody's life, he didn't do anything. He was a nonentity, as most people are."

I thank the Screenwriter for his time, wish him good luck, and head for home. How easy it is, to take the routine incidents of the day for granted, but in the car I make an effort to see everything with a fresh eye. A red light changing to green, a chocolate-brown UPS truck, ice-laminated trees melting in the sunlight, a bumper sticker on a Toyota stuck in the ditch: DIE TRYING.

THE CRUSADER is downloading a batch of e-mail when I arrive, so she invites me to sit in an overstuffed black lounge chair in front of a giant-screen television while I wait. A little terrier trots out and gives me a curious look. There's a stack of videos beside the TV, topped off with a copy of *Harold and Maude,* a black comedy about an old lady and a funeral-obsessed rich kid who keeps acting out mock suicides. This must be the place.

I first heard the Crusader on a radio talk show about funerals. The show was produced in New Hampshire, where the Senate was considering a bill to grant family members and designated agents the right to handle funeral details such as death records, body transportation, and burial permits. The existing statute reserved those tasks for licensed undertakers, which the Crusader argued denied people a traditional and often therapeutic involvement in family funerals, as well as creating unfair funeral costs. She'd been invited to appear on the show as head of the Funeral and Memorial Society Association of America and as author of *Caring for the Dead,* a do-it-yourself about funeral procedures. She shared the mike with the head of the New Hampshire Undertakers and Embalmers Association, and it was a feisty debate, with the Crusader making a persuasive case for the new law, and the funeral director making predictable pitches for the benefits of his services, including cosmetic embalming, upholstered caskets, and the comforts of a funeral-parlor organist or tasteful (and economical) CD.

Most callers were sympathetic to the proposed law, though some didn't like the idea of people driving dead bodies around in their SUVs. Weren't there health risks and a potential for disease? Nothing a twenty-five-cent pair of latex gloves couldn't stop, the Crusader curtly replied. Another caller was alarmed about the criminal possibilities. Think how easy it would be to overdose your grandmother, drive her off to the crematory, and pocket the insurance. The Crusader pointed out that New Hampshire was one of only six states that didn't already allow such liberties, and there had been no indication that disease or crime was rampant.

As it turned out, the funeral industry declined to take an official position on the statute, for fear of being seen as self-serving, and the law passed.

The Crusader sounded like someone who might understand my quest. She talked about being compelled to have a do-it-yourself funeral for her first husband to save money, and about finding that the emotional benefits were even more valuable than the financial ones. Subsequent family deaths had been followed with homemade funerals, and not because of the economics. She is a believer.

"Mind if I smoke?" she asks, sitting on the couch beside my chair. The dog jumps up beside her and snuggles tight.

"Go ahead." I've learned that a good way to have a lousy conversation with smokers is to cut off their nicotine. The Crusader lights up and settles in. She's wearing a black turtleneck and dark sweat pants. Black hair cut short. A tough north-country woman.

When I called I told her I was interested in funeral practices and in understanding why we'd inherited such a schizophrenic culture. Lots of violence and death in our entertainment, but little stomach for the real thing. I wondered where her organization fit in. There'd been a few deaths in my hometown recently, and I'd heard from several survivors who wished they'd taken a more hands-on approach. In the end, they'd left it up to the professionals and felt vaguely unfulfilled, not to mention shortchanged.

"Memorial societies have been the world's best-kept secret for years," she says. "They started back in the late 1930s after the Depression. A radical Unitarian minister in Seattle was appalled at the high cost of dying, when the industry was pushing embalming and manufactured caskets. He represented a group of people who went to a funeral director and said, We don't think a funeral should cost more than such and such, we want a simple exit, no frills. If we send all our members to you, will you agree to honor this price? That was how the first urban memorial society started. It was not inconsistent with some of the thoughts behind the old burial co-ops in the agrarian Midwest and the burial societies of the South. Each one has a slightly different flavor, but a similar concern. How do we prepare for the end of life without spending a lot of money?"

I ask her how we got into a situation where paying through the nose for funerals is the norm, and she backtracks to pioneer America, when a group of women would come to the deceased's house and help with the laying out of the dead. Later, during the Victorian era, there would often be an elaborate laying out in the front parlor, with the body on display surrounded by fancy draperies. Funeral photos were taken, "beautiful memory pictures" that can be seen in collections today. But as we became a more dispersed society, there wasn't room or time to lay grandma out in the parlor anymore. We were spreading out, and the funeral moved from the family home to the undertaker's "home." We lost the common lore of what to do at a time of death.

"But the public have been willing victims in this," the Crusader points out. "There's a lot of superstitious thinking. If we talk about it, it might happen. Or, I don't want to seem morbid. I know my grandmother tried to talk to me about her funeral thoughts when I was in my twenties and I was very uncomfortable. I said, Oh Grammy, you're not going to die, and I wouldn't let her talk about it and she didn't insist. That was the sad thing. In hindsight I wish she had insisted."

The Crusader tells me that according to the Federal Trade Commission, the average person arranges for one funeral in a lifetime. No wonder we often don't get it right. Not enough practice. This is where the memorial societies came in, spreading up and down the west coast, across the

U.S., and up into Canada. Eventually, in the 1960s, Jessica Mitford got involved, and with the publication of *The American Way of Death*, the movement got a big push. In 1963 a national organization was formed, and members succeeded in bringing down the cost of their own funerals. But the movement, marginal at best, was an easy target. Some of the affiliated funeral directors became isolated professionally for participating in funeral societies, which were seen as communist organizations.

"Jessica was an out-and-out Communist," the Crusader admits of Mitford, "and it was very difficult for our groups to get nonprofit status. She would get annoyed when members didn't have a larger sense of activism. She called memorial-society people a bunch of eggheads, Unitarians, Quakers, and old farts who were nothing more than middlemen for the industry. On the one hand, she would promote them, because she thought it was awful that the undertakers were charging so much, but she would get annoyed. . . . She wanted them to be more socially active. And many of them were merely acting as cooperative buyers' clubs. Once they had a cheap funeral for themselves, that's all they cared about."

By the early 1980s, the societies succeeded in pressuring the FTC into passing funeral regulations requiring certain consumer rights, including written disclosure of price information, a list of sixteen basic services, and a package price for immediate cremation, including a minimum alternative container, which usually meant a cardboard box. Once the funeral rules went into effect, some of the societies thought they'd gotten everything they needed, and believed that people would now be allowed to pick and choose only the services they wanted. Membership dwindled and some societies disbanded. The narrow focus that bothered Mitford very nearly killed off the movement.

IN 1987, the Crusader published her first book, *Caring for Your Own Dead* (followed ten years later by *Caring for the Dead: Your Final Act of Love*). Essentially a funeral "how-to" guide, it was inspired by a series of family deaths during the 1980s, beginning with the suicide of her husband. With two young children and next to nothing in the bank, she was forced to scrutinize every budget item in the funeral plan, and wound up putting together a homemade version, including transport of the body to the crematory. As she discovered, it wasn't the financial savings that proved most significant.

"That the total cost would now be under $200 had become secondary," she wrote. "I needed to be a part of John's death as I was of his life. If I had had the money, I would have lost that—given that away—in a moment of grief and confusion."

The book presented detailed information on legal and hygienic requirements in every state, and a persuasive argument for getting involved in family funerals. People began calling her for help, not only survivors and those preparing their own funeral plans, but also a chapter of the Funeral and Memorial Society of America. Several local societies had not found a low-cost funeral provider and were looking for help bypassing the professionals entirely. It wasn't long before they asked her to get involved in running the national organization. She began as a board member, and in the process of researching the group's background, came to the conclusion that FAMSA had an identity crisis.

"It was not clear who we were," she recalls. "People thought FAMSA was part of the funeral industry. Half the people on the board looked like a good case of embalming. They didn't have a vision. Probably ninety percent of memorial-society people opt for cremation, and consequently they are seen as cremation societies, when in fact they started out as a simplicity society. They were really pro–consumer choice."

The Crusader began by improving the visibility of the organization. She was profiled in a cover story in *U.S. News and World Report* headlined "Don't Die Before You Read This," which I read in a physician's waiting room. She got mentions in Ann Landers and Dear Abby and appeared twice on *Donahue*. "After Dear Abby and Ann Landers, we got thirty thousand pieces of mail," she says. "They had to pull in volunteers to handle it all."

I ask her what a member gets for the one-time $25 fee. "The active societies have done a funeral-price survey in their area and/or negotiated a discount for certain cooperating funeral homes. Definitely as a member you're going to get the cheapest funeral around. It saves hundreds of dollars. The societies have reciprocal arrangements, so if you die away from home there's a good chance you'll be eligible to use a cooperating funeral home wherever you are."

She explains that the organization consists of 120 societies across the country, totalling about five hundred thousand members. Seattle has almost one hundred thousand members and a paid staff, whereas some local societies struggle with a volunteer staff, administered off of someone's kitchen table. FAMSA has a predominately urban membership, and with recent staff changes is becoming more progressive and socially active.

In 1999, the Crusader was appointed Executive Director of FAMSA, and the first thing she did was change the name to the Funeral Consumer's Alliance. "Anyone can get behind a consumer's right to choose," she says, recalling a speech she gave to the alliance. "I told them, If the industry did not manipulate the grieving, did not hide the low-cost caskets, did not dominate the funeral boards with self-serving regulations, did not limit who could sell caskets or in what states you could care for your own dead, there would be no need for our organization. But we have an obligation to protect the public at large, not just our members. It absolutely electrified the whole audience. There was suddenly a new reason to do what we're doing."

Research in the society files turned up an old survey that indicated that people resented proselytizing for low-budget funerals. Instead, they wanted to know their options. "The discount might be influential, but only so-so. Information was what they wanted, and that's what we do. We have an 800-number, we have free materials on the Internet. We're not in this to make money, it's a nonprofit outfit. And when we get at-need calls, which we get all the time, the first question we ask is what funeral rituals are important to your family."

I remind the Crusader that in our death-denying society there may not be any funeral rituals. That was the problem I faced at the start of my quest. Building a coffin looked like a plausible way to fill an empty hole.

"Building your own coffin is not for everyone," she laughs. "I suggest that people sit down and talk to family members and find out what's going to be important to them, too. Let them know what your druthers are, because most people want to honor the wishes of the deceased. One old gentleman who had planned to donate his body to a medical school suddenly discovered that he had a daughter who had a really hard time with that, and so he made alternative plans out of deference to her resistance. Sometimes the idea of cremation is not acceptable to the family. Sometimes the idea of embalming is not acceptable. So these are things that need to be talked about ahead of time. And in some respects I think it's been unfortunate that people do *too much* planning ahead. There really is something very therapeutic to survivors to be actively involved. I've heard people say it was wonderful, my father had everything arranged, it was one call to the funeral director and he did everything. But that's almost too bad, almost too bad." She pauses to light another cigarette. "I know that when my father was in his final weeks I sat down and wrote an obituary and e-mailed it to my three brothers, one of whom I'm not very friendly with—God the doctor." She laughs. "And yet he made some wonderful contributions to the obituary. He added things I'd forgotten about or things that he knew about and I didn't. And it became a much nicer tribute to our father because we shared in that process. And yet other people will write their own obituaries highlighting what they want to be known for, which I think is an exercise in arrogance. How dare you tell the rest of the world how we should remember you? That should be something we as survivors decide. People who teach classes on death and dying invariably ask class students to plan their own funeral, when the really difficult task is planning a funeral for someone close to you. I've had instructors say, Oh, that would be too difficult. Well, give me a fucking break! That's the point! Now you're getting smart."

There it is again, the conflicted American attitude toward death. We teach our kids about money, politics, religion, maybe even sex, but we don't do a very good job teaching them about death, dying, and funerals.

A striking example of this can be found in the public discussion of these questions. "Right now there is megabucks in grant money floating around in end-of-life issues," the Crusader says. "Robert Wood Johnson and the George Soros Foundation. And yet they barely tolerate us trying to get involved in these projects. They talk about the quality of life and how we die, then they leap over the dead body and jump into bereavement as if there is no connection. I find that very *schizzy*. They do not want to talk about dead bodies. Yet I'm convinced on a personal level—and I would say not just me, but anyone else I know who's had a hands-on funeral experience—that it's far easier to accept the death; the bereavement time is diminished considerably, because you've had this loving and therapeutic experience that is very cathartic."

The Crusader's first such experience came with her husband's suicide in 1981. Thirty-one years old, he had been suffering from chronic stomach pain, and ended it one night with a rifle in the front seat of his pickup. The Crusader says that her involvement with his funeral, from the moment she discovered his body to burying his ashes in a flower garden, was curative. "It was much easier for me to let go," she recalls, "because he looked dead. If he had been returned to a lifelike condition with the embalmer's magic I would have bargained with God to wake him up. I remember we drove his body to the crematory and when we got there I wanted to see the body one more time. The need was very strong. We got a screwdriver out from under the front seat of the truck and took the screws out and because John looked dead, I was ready to let go. I remember that as a very distinct and a very profound feeling."

I ask the Crusader what she thinks about open-casket viewing. Is it healthy or counterproductive? She replies that the only people who feel a need to see the body tend to be the immediate family, not neighbors and co-workers, unless they are especially close friends. In the case of an anticipated death, people have already started saying their goodbyes. With an unanticipated death, there is a much greater need to come to grips with the reality of death. What about kids?

"I think kids should be given a choice. They will let you know." She adds that the funeral industry is not consistent about what viewing means, and at what times in the process you see the body. "People ought to realize they have a choice, viewing vs. visitation, funeral vs. memorial, church vs. funeral parlor."

I recall discussing some of these options with the Undertaker, who cheerfully suggested that there are as many ways to go as there are different personalities. Technically, though, viewing involves actually displaying the body in an open coffin. Visitation, or calling hours, reserves a special time before the service for members of the family and perhaps friends to gather and lend each other support; this could take place before the service, or the night before, and can be scheduled with services or memorials with either closed or open casket, or no casket at all, in case of cremation. The funeral itself is associated with an actual burial, and can take place at a church, funeral home, graveside, Elks Club, home, or just about anywhere imaginable. On the other hand, a memorial service is held after cremation. If a body cannot be buried during the winter in frozen ground, there may be a graveside service the following spring at the interment.

I suggest that given all these choices, on top of the emotional stress of dealing with death, it's no wonder people leave the whole business to the funeral director.

"The conscientious, sensitive funeral director will help educate you," she says. "On the other hand, they will also very willingly let you turn it over to them, and they will plan a more expensive one. The problem is that there are too many undertakers that expect full-time pay for part-time work. Years ago it was a sideline. Now they crank the prices up to charge you waiting-around-until-you-die time. I wouldn't mind that there are too many, but there are too many who aren't refinishing antiques, or making wooden toys, or something on the side that could be interrupted when you get a call. Funeral directors feel they have to live up to an image, a certain kind of car, paint on the house. But the majority of funeral homes in Vermont are doing fifty calls a year. One a week. It really goes back to economics. When you're a funeral home and you're sweating your mortgage it's a situation that invites abuse."

She reminds me of several recent scandals in the state involving funeral directors convicted of fraud. One was discovered selling expensive caskets and then using cheap models for the actual burial; bodies were even piled up in his garage. Another coerced grieving survivors into buying unwanted services. Preneed funds disappeared after one undertaker went bankrupt. "In any other business, when you've got too many suppliers the prices go down. In this business, they go up. Figure that."

Financial pressures have made many of the independent funeral homes easy picking for corporate buyouts, which triggers alarms for the Crusader. "We know from reports that the manipulative sales tactics of these giant chains are pretty despicable. All they really care about is the stockholders, not the neighborhood family. Their whole priority shifts when it's owned by a Wall Street company. Not to mention that a lot of those stocks are in the toilet."

She told me about a woman who belonged to a memorial society in the Midwest. After her death, it turned out that the cooperating funeral home had been bought out by SCI, a large funeral chain. They tried to add $250 to the previously contracted fee, and when the woman's son objected, they wouldn't release the ashes. The son called the Crusader.

"He was ripshit," she recalls. "He faxed me his material and I Fed-Exed it to the FTC. Three days, and I got an opinion back. I never got an opinion so fast. It's illegal."

Despite these horror stories, the Crusader foresees a positive future for consumers. "Look at the generation that demanded we recycle. Many of them write their own wedding vows. They demanded the right to natural childbirth and home schooling. I think they are going to take charge of their funeral experience, just the way you're taking charge."

For example, she says, there is a very strong "green burial" movement in England. No embalming, no vaults, biodegradable coffins, natural stone markers. She's heard from a doctor starting a green burial ground in South Carolina, as well as Muslim groups who are establishing special cemeteries to suit their religious beliefs.

She also foresees the cremation rate rising dramatically, and this trend may mean the demise of overpriced funeral services. "I think the prediction of the cremation rate is way too low. They're talking forty percent in ten years. It's already twenty-five percent. I think it'll be closer to seventy percent in ten years. The Kennedy-Bissette choice is going to free up a lot of Catholics. Vermont has a very high cremation rate, thirty-six percent. But I was talking to a funeral director in North Carolina, Deep South we're talking, and he said forty percent of his preneed is cremation. In fact, the majority of funeral directors opt for cremation themselves."

Another positive trend is the increase in female undertakers. Forty percent of the mortuary classes are women, a huge increase in a traditionally male business. "The commercial funeral business started out as a male-dominated industry. Embalming, casket making, gravedigging. But caring for the dead had been a female-dominated task, and now the blending of caring for the dead and funeral rituals is being better balanced."

These optimistic curves are offset by what the Crusader perceives as one of her biggest challenges. She says that her late father-in-law spent his last days in the lounge chair I'm sitting in, trying to follow the storyline on the big screen. "Toward the end he got agitated, and I had to ask for stronger medication. The dose the doctor had prescribed was too low, and I felt like a criminal putting on a second morphine patch at night. Finally we got the liquid form. So one of my major concerns right now is comfort care at the end of life. I'm sure Charlie wouldn't have gotten the right prescription if I had not intervened and demanded it. That makes me angry as hell. If you've got a living will, durable power of attorney for health care, you better find a witch on wheels to name as your surrogate, because unless you've got an aggressive family member or agent, the medical profession won't listen at all. Robert Wood Johnson spent fifty-six million dollars and documented the fact that the medical profession was not honoring wills unless there was an aggressive relative."

The Crusader adds that hospice organizations also need reform. "We have a very hard time reaching hospice," she says. "Isn't that ironic? They're really geared to hands-on care of the dying, but they don't want to hear about caring for your own dead." I tell the Crusader it's hard to believe an organization so intimate with death would be in denial. She shakes her head. "They're not in denial, they're in bed with the industry. Sometimes funeral directors donate the most money to the local hospice program. They're on the hospice boards. One hospice center in Ohio wasn't allowed to distribute our memorial society materials with low-cost alternatives because the funeral director on the board of the hospice objected. So find out, does your hospice have its own agenda for which funeral director you ought to call? We haven't finished sorting out the politics of death."

I suggest that if the politics of death is anything like the politics of life, I won't be holding my breath waiting for the truth and sanity to shake out. Not with Dr. Kevorkian in jail, billboards begging for organ donors, and drug companies scrambling for the fountain-of-youth pill. The Crusader smiles. All in due time. Meanwhile, she's putting in eighty hours a week coaching grieving survivors, doing interviews, running the Funeral Consumer's Alliance website, and putting together a book of funeral humor.

"It's to help break the ice," she says. "So families can begin to discuss the subject without scaring everybody. It's loaded with little sidebars of useful information, but the book itself is very light. Joan Rivers said, I had to take my mother-in-law to the crematory today. Someone responded, Oh? Rough day I guess. Yeah, she didn't want to go!" She laughs and remembers another one about Vermont legend Ethan Allen. "Ethan Allen on his deathbed was told the angels are waiting. The angels are waiting? The angels are waiting? Well, goddamn 'em, let 'em wait!"

The phone rings and it's time for the Crusader to do a talk show with a radio station in San Antonio. It's hard not to be impressed, even a shade awe-struck, with a woman who is wrestling overtime with life's biggest bummer. Some have criticized the Crusader for being hot tempered, pushy, inflexible. But if that's what it takes to wake a culture in denial, so be it. I thank her and put on my coat, feeling more resolute than when I arrived, but glad to be heading home.

GINSENG is rumored to be at rest here in the Ridgewell Cemetery in Guildhall, Vermont, but after walking the burying ground, there's no sign of his gravestone. Born George Willard, he acquired the nickname because of his uncanny skill at rooting out the elusive medicinal herb and selling it for a tidy profit, and now he's playing as hard to get as his wild-woods namesake. He was also a tough woodsman and teamster, but he's best remembered for the coffin he built and slept in for two years, "to make sure it fit." Or so the story goes.

I hike past row after row of dull gray monuments looking for the old-timer while a solitary crow squawks at me from a pine tree near the gate. Perfect casting. The late February sun is warm and bright, and the thin crust of snow makes for easy walking and an efficient record of the graves I've already checked. The snow is undisturbed by other visitors.

Across Route 102 the Connecticut River flows south under a shell of gray ice, and not far beyond, the White Mountains shoulder up against a flat, blue sky. Occasionally a truck loaded with timber roars north, twenty-two big wheels grinding up slush, bound for the sawmills in Quebec. Somewhere in this cemetery lies a man who spent his life doing the very same thing, hauling logs, only he drove them with a team of draft horses. Now he's spending eternity listening to the pounding of trucks instead of hoofbeats.

I've driven north because I'm sick of winter. Around this time of year old folks sometimes wander off into the woods to die, preferring a quick exit to insulting cell-by-cell disintegration. I've heard that freezing to death is painless, that cold is nature's morphine. Who knows. I do believe that to overcome an obstacle, you must confront it. Instead of fleeing south, I delve in deeper.

The Northeast Kingdom reminds me why I live in a state known for six-month winters and six months of tough sledding. The Kingdom is the way America used to be. Rickety old houses, dirt roads, sprawling forests, mountains without cell-phone towers or ski lifts, and ghosts. It's the home of the Dowsers' Society, an organization representing the world's water witches, who find water with a forked stick and missing souls with a crystal. Just up the road from this cemetery, Abenaki Indians made pilgrimages to the Brunswick mineral springs for healing, but always during the day. They never camped overnight. The spirits, they believed, had a demonic side. Roger's Rangers escaped across these bogs after destroying an Indian village in Quebec, one of the most harrowing journeys in colonial history. In *Northwest Passage,* Kenneth Roberts dramatized the march through a land possessed. "If there is worse country— for men in a hurry—than to the east of Memphremagog, I have yet to see it," the narrator recalls.

> . . . its hills and mountains are packed together like fish balls on a platter; and wind, blowing between two hills and striking another, is twisted about so that it blows in circles. . . . As for the watercourses, there are brooks within half a mile of each other, flowing in four directions at the same time . . . and the valleys through which some of them flow are so deep and so involved that they seem to have been planned and dug by an insane god.

Around here nature refuses to be paved over, tamed, denied. Much like Ginseng—a man one of his neighbors described as an outstanding example of "God's carelessness."

THIS IS WHAT I know about Ginseng. He lived in Guildhall. He was a teamster and logger who worked for the Connecticut Valley Lumber Company sometime before and after the turn of the twentieth century. In addition to digging up ginseng roots, he collected and sold spruce gum, the woodsman's Wrigley's. He built a miniature western stagecoach, complete with model driver, armed guard, and passengers. He hunted and trapped throughout the northwoods from Vermont to Maine, and proudly wore a necklace of one hundred porcupine claws and a rakish wide-brimmed felt hat, an outfit Major Rogers no doubt would have admired. He built a dancehall, nailed a stuffed bobcat head over the door, and sold tickets to Saturday-night junkets. One morning his wife refused to get out of bed and make him breakfast, so he threw a bucket of ice water on her. She left. He wrote poetry.

I came across these stories about Ginseng in Robert Pike's histories of northwoods logging lore, *Tall Trees, Tough Men* and *Spiked Boots*. Pike befriended Ginseng, listened to his tales, and snapped a photo of the old logger standing beside the coffin he'd supposedly fashioned out of a rosewood piano. The books were published decades ago, and by the time I read them I figured Ginseng was long dead. I had no idea when he died, or where he and his coffin wound up, but I made a few calls and tracked down a woman named Peg Rogers who'd written a history of Guildhall. I asked her if she'd known Ginseng.

"No, that was before my time," she said, adding that she knew little more than what she'd also read in Pike's books. Did she know where he was buried? She suggested the Ridgewell Cemetery. She also gave me the names of a couple of Ginseng's relatives, two great-grandnieces descended from his sister. I called Helen Boswell, and by chance her sister Elizabeth Odell was visiting, so I asked them what they remembered.

"George Willard? Oh, yes," Elizabeth Odell recalled. "We used to stop by all the time. My father used to go with him collecting ginseng. He lived out on the North Road, but the house and the dance hall are gone now. He used to tell us stories." She laughed. "I think he tried to scare us." Did she remember the rosewood coffin? "Yes," she said, "but it wasn't made out of a piano. I think it was made out of a candy case, so he could see out." She added something else that wasn't in either of Pike's books. "You know, he dug his own grave in the front yard, but the town wouldn't let him be buried in it."

Trekking back and forth across the cemetery, I wonder which story to believe. The coffin was made out of a rosewood piano. It was made out of a candy case. Ginseng dug his own grave. He was buried in the Ridgewell Cemetery. I retrace my steps. Still no luck. The crow flies away with a disgusted croak. Near the cemetery fence I find a fresh grave and a dark granite headstone decorated with an eerie image of the Connecticut River under a jet black rainbow. I think of the film *Black Rainbow,* a supernatural thriller about a phony psychic who suddenly finds her predictions coming true. Unfortunately, all she can predict is death, which doesn't do much for her popularity. I wonder what people driving by will think of a stranger wandering around their village cemetery. Suddenly this quest to overcome death seems nuts. Death is death, nobody's going to overcome it, why not forget about it and get on with living?

But instead of heading home, I drive north into the village of Guildhall. Is it because I've come too far to turn back now? Is the story taking over, mesmerizing as the unruly landscape? I think it's simply that I'm hoping that Ginseng's final wishes weren't ignored. Whether it was a candy case or a rosewood piano, if he's got to listen to diesel trucks roaring through eternity, let it be in his own homemade box.

I pull over in town, a few white-clapboard colonials and a library. Not a soul in sight. The place looks abandoned, a ghost town with all the residents in the cemetery. Strange, for a town that's the county seat, with a school and a courthouse. I circle the green looking for the Town Hall where I'm hoping to find a record of burials. Still no people. Not even a crow.

I find a sign for the Essex County Court. Hoping to get directions to the Town Hall, I walk up the wheelchair ramp and open the door. A woman in a police uniform sits next to the door to the courtroom. She gives me a look as cold as the frozen river outside. She's wearing a holstered black pistol.

"Go through the metal detector," she says.

"I'm looking for the Town House," I tell her, not moving.

"It's on the corner," she says in a flat monotone. "It's not open today. It's open next week. Tuesday."

She's beautiful, a raven-haired knockout, but her eyes are ice. As I walk out I think I know why. Two years ago, across the river in Colebrook, a man named Carl Drega started shooting people and he didn't stop until the police gunned him down in Vermont, just north of here, close to the mineral springs the Abenaki revere and fear. Five killed, including a female judge, a newspaper editor, and two New Hampshire state troopers, and several more wounded. The Kingdom may look the way it used to be, but it's up-to-date in paranoia.

Suddenly cemeteries don't seem so appealing. You could build a hundred coffins and never get over that kind of dying. Yes, indeed, it's time to go home. But hang in there, Ginseng, I'll be back.

THE ORGANIST flicks on the power switch and plays the opening notes of a Bach cantata. He's a big man and his hands span two octaves on the small organ keyboard. I hit a couple of notes and flinch. The keys are ice cold. The church sanctuary isn't heated during the week, and the Organist tells me that sometimes when he plays there's frost on the wall next to the organ pipes. Outside, a raw March wind is blowing snow devils around the churchyard. I've come to discuss funeral music with the Organist. We've had an unusually high number of deaths in town this winter, and the funeral services have featured a wide range of music, from "Amazing Grace" to *Grand Canyon Suite*. I like to think that the deceased had some influence on the choice of music, but then again, who knows? The music may be for the living, but I'd hate to be hovering over this church during my own service with hands over my ears.

The Organist tells me that his predecessor was a woman who laid a rug over the pedals when she played to keep the cold from chilling her nether parts. "Without the bass notes," he says, "it sounded like a calliope." He clicks off the organ and we leave the sanctuary for the comfort of the heated study.

I tell the Organist about the funeral that began with the *Grand Canyon Suite,* conducted at a church down the road, and how the pastor had to walk the length of the altar after everyone was seated to shut off the CD player. It was somewhere between "On The Trail" and "Sunset," and it took her an awkward minute to find the switch. I think I'd prefer a live soloist to a canned orchestra. I ask him what kind of music he recommends for funerals.

"It depends on the individual, the family," he says. "Anything from a reflective type of service where it's meditative, to tried-and-true hymns like "The Old Rugged Cross." I always try to start with quiet organ music for people coming in, because there is going to be talking going on. I don't want to be blasting them out so they can't hear, and I also feel it's more respectful to the family and the dead. Some Bach Chorales, a couple of Liszt pieces, Rachmaninov, Handel, Wagner adaptations of hymns. It depends on what kind of service you want."

The Organist has been playing church organ since he was a teenager growing up in the Northeast Kingdom. After distinguishing himself on the piano, he was recruited to fill in for ill or vacationing organists in all three churches in town. "Obviously, with all those churches, weddings and funerals came up, and if I was the only show in town, I got the call. I remember the first funeral I had, for the Episcopal church. They're very ritualistic, there was a lot of ceremony and incense and bells and chanting, and it was pretty much all laid out what I was supposed to do. No Scott Joplin," he laughs. "Today you could get away with ragtime."

Early personal encounters with death jaded the Organist's feelings about mourning. His father died when he was thirteen, two grandparents not long after, and he lost several high school friends to car accidents, illness, and Vietnam. "Within a period of a couple of years, funerals were just such a personal part of my life, so that I got a rather cynical view. Then as I got older and started to raise a family of my own, I started to realize it's not what's in the box that matters. It's what the person has left for you."

The Organist tells me that funeral plans usually begin with a call from the local undertaker, someone he's worked with many times during his twenty years as church musical director. They discuss the families' requests and work out a program. "I have a standard package, so to speak, it's usually ten to fifteen minutes of quiet prelude-type music, hymn singing during the service, and whatever afterwards, enough to get them out of the building. It's basically for a half hour's worth of work. If there are special requests, things to hunt up, I will charge accordingly. And there are times when I don't charge anything, I would do it simply for the family, local friends. I consider that my gift to the family. And with others, I wish to hell I'd charged them a fortune, because they put you through the tortures of the damned. We had one a couple of years ago—during the postlude after the service the casket stayed open the whole time and at the end the family were throwing themselves on the body, they were putting little kids up, kiss Grandmother goodbye! I'm sorry, I mean that kid's gonna have nightmares, and they're gonna have major psychology bills in the future. I just don't think that's good for the family. The person is dead, they know the person is dead, they've had their time for grieving at home, and I think it should be a way of saying goodbye, some closure."

I remind the Organist that open-casket viewing was a long-standing New England tradition, back when closure was literal—the moment the lid was nailed down. The open casket at a funeral service, whether at home or in a church, was essential to the grieving process. People touched the body, children were lifted for one last kiss, and sometimes an hysterical mourner would try to drag the corpse out of the coffin. In fact, it was considered good luck to touch a corpse and, contrary to the Organist's opinion, essential to preventing nightmares about the dead person. Exaggerated mourning allowed people to vent repressed grief or even to feel depths of sadness that might not have been there to begin with. Either way, public grief was considered useful, and a ceremony that didn't include a lot of weeping and wailing was considered a terrible disappointment.

The Organist shakes his head. "No, when I go I want some space in there. I want a couple of months to go by, then have the memorial. I don't want to be around. I don't even want an urn there. Because I'm going to be there anyway. The person that dies is in the hearts and minds of the people who are present and that is all you need. Because I will be damned if I'm going to put my family through what I've seen some of these other families go through. My family knows I want to be cremated ASAP, and they've agreed. It's my personal feeling, but I feel that funeral is a misnomer. It should be a celebration of a person's life, not a rending of garments and weeping and gnashing of teeth. I want people to remember me as an alive person, not this piece of meat in a box. That's where I object to the open casket. It's almost like idolatry. Because that to me is not a person. That urn of ashes is not a person. The person is in your heart and in your head. And however they have touched your lives, that's how they should be remembered. If it were up to me, I'd put funeral directors out of business."

In fact, making a career of playing overwrought funerals might be downright unhealthy. The Organist is recovering from a heart attack. I ask him about the emotional toll of playing two or three dozen funerals a year for twenty years. He grimaces. "Sure, there are times when I will actually get caught up in the emotion of it. There was one for a twelve-year-old girl who got hit by a car that was driven by her uncle. On Halloween! That was something I never want to go through again. There have been times when I'm in the middle of something and I wished I'd gotten someone else to do this job, it was too much, a service for a close friend in the community. But I make it through. It's a hard business if you're any kind of a human being. Sure, you're going to have these musical monkeys that'll go in and crank out music for funeral after funeral after funeral and it's simply routine. But if I ever get to that point I'm going to quit."

Since the Organist's heart attack three years ago, he's had to give up cigarettes and change his diet. His outlook on life has also changed. "When I got out of the hospital, the first thing I did was go to the lawyer and we drew up a living will and I specified what would and would not be done with me. As far as funeral services go, I don't know if it's because I've had an appreciable brush with the inevitable, but I now have more of an appreciation of what-all is going on there. It's weird, really, but it's also great. Every day I get up really is a gift, and I try to look at it that way. That's the way I want to live my life, and that's the way I want to end my life when the end comes."

I ask the Organist what kind of music he wants played at his own funeral. "'Amazing Grace,'" he replies, without missing a beat. "I love that, I want it done on bagpipes. It's one of my favorites. As a matter of fact, that one turned up this week at the last funeral I did. I played just the one finger melody, with a two-note drone on the bottom that stays right through, and it came out rather well, I surprised even myself. It's like that wail you hear on the bagpipe. It's a neat little trick I might use again."

That's the magic of the organ, variable as a musical chameleon, shifting from breathy flute to bass drum, cymbal to cannon shot, bird call to storming thunder. It's the original synthesizer. The first organs appeared in early Greece and Rome, huge outdoor pipes powered by manually operated bellows and hydraulic pistons. Some organs required as many as seventy men to pump out the sound. They were used as sirens to summon people to festivals, weddings, and funerals. As these "noise machines" became more sophisticated, royal courts found them essential to their decadent romps. An organ, not a fiddle, was Nero's favorite instrument, and in the Roman circuses they were used to sound the execution signal for condemned Christians. Ironically, like many other pagan devices, the organ was eventually adopted by the Christian church. The great cathedrals of medieval Europe competed with each other for the finest *organum,* and for many years the church banned all other instruments from its services.

Scholarly histories of the organ offer varying explanations for the church's singular allegiance to the instrument. Some suggest it was because of the organ's usefulness in teaching musical composition; others that it was simply the ultimate gadget of the time. There's no doubt that the heavenly oriented pipes could fill a cathedral with sound and awe. But there's also something about organ music and death that go hand in hand, like those medieval portraits of hurdy-gurdy–cranking skeletons leading the *Totentanz,* dance of death. In many churches, those moaning, mournful pipes were reserved for funerals only. No other instrument so convincingly conjures up the sound of doom.

Why else would the organ be used in so many Gothic mysteries and horror films, not only for the score, but often as the protagonist's favorite instrument and musical alter ego? In the original *Phantom of the Opera,* Lon Chaney's disfigured Count dashes to the keyboard to vent his anguish, rage, and mad delight, and the phallic throb of his pipes is demented and hilarious. No wonder early Latin church clergy called the organist "the pulsator." The heroine of the 1960s drive-in classic *Carnival of Souls* is a lonely, repressed church organist whose life closes in on her until one day she discovers strange ecstasies playing in her bare feet. Nero would have understood, but in prefeminist America, this meant big trouble, and she wound up at the bottom of a river. And some of the silent films that first screened with a live organist are now scored for that instrument on video. One of the most haunting is Timothy Green's sound track for Murnau's vampire classic, *Nosferatu.*

I can imagine the Organist laying down a horror music soundtrack at my funeral, but somehow I don't think my family would appreciate the joke. Better play it straight. One "Amazing Grace" coming up, hold the bagpipes. A two-note drone on the organ will do just fine. I tell the Organist to keep it lively, and he nods.

"I make it a point not to drag out the hymns so they sound like dirges," he says. "I keep them upbeat. I really don't want people just sitting there weeping into their hankies." He tells me to put a list of music together when I get a chance. There's a moment of cold silence. "No hurry, of course."

THE FLORIST stands in the cooler surveying a dim room full of cold flowers. He picks out a dozen red roses and steps back into the warmth of the flower shop, where he trims the stems and mixes the bouquet with a spray of ostrich ferns. Flecks of greenery stick to his perspiring face and his glasses. He wraps the stems in moist paper and plastic, and bundles the bouquet in white tissue. It's a wedding-anniversary present for his customer's wife, and the brass sleigh bells over the door jingle when he leaves.

It's early April. In Vermont that means a tug of war between winter and spring, and today, outside, you'd have to call it a draw, with the sun and clouds pulling in both directions. But inside the shop spring has arrived. The greenhouse is jungle warm, and white styrofoam trays of bedding plants are sprouting tomatoes, peppers, leeks, broccoli, cabbage, nasturtiums, and marigolds.

This is the Florist's busiest season, and he warns me that he hasn't got much time to answer questions about memorial flowers, but then again funeral sales do add up to fifty percent of his income and in a competitive business he may see me as a customer he can't afford to lose. He asks me to stay while he works.

I let him know that I'm dealing with funeral issues ahead of time so my family will have some idea how to handle my service. It had never occurred to me to think about flowers until I found myself increasingly drawn to the newspaper's obituary section, taking daily satisfaction in outliving whatever poor soul happened to buy the farm, and puzzling over those popular concluding refrains, "In lieu of flowers . . ." and "Please Omit." Why do people ban flowers from their funerals? I recalled the Organist's scorn for lavish funeral flower baskets. Is this a rebellion against expensive funeral undertakings, is there something immodest about flowers, or is it a selfless way to divert money to the deceased's favorite charity? Perhaps some people are simply allergic.

"I hate that," says the Florist, shaking his head. "I've had families come in and order a lot of flowers and yet still have 'Please Omit' or 'In lieu of . . .' in the obituary. The problem I have with those two terms is—not everybody will read the obituary. And it's not my job to check the obituary and tell everybody that they don't want flowers. So we'll have people order flowers. Yet nobody else ordered flowers. We take the flowers down, and their flower arrangement is the only one in the church." The Florist grimaces. "To me it should be a decision of what people want to do themselves."

The Florist tells me that his shop has been in the family for three generations, beginning with his grandfather. He remembers a story his father told about a prominent family in town that experienced a death, and a lot of people ordered sympathy flowers. "He had about twenty different floral pieces that he took down to the church, and the woman whose mother had died did not want flowers, so she would not let him bring flowers into the church. In fact, the ones he brought in she purposely took and tossed them outside. All the cards that were on there, which normally the family will respond to, were lost. So my father had all these people calling him up and saying, You delivered the flowers down there, right? Did you deliver the flowers? Because she never responded to anybody, which was a bad situation." The way the Florist tells the story, "bad situation" sounds like an understatement. He seems worried that it might happen again. "The way we've arranged for it now, the undertaker will not put 'In lieu of . . .' unless a family downright insists on it. What they'll put instead is nothing, or say memorial contributions can be accepted, and just leave the 'In lieu of . . .' out."

What about the flower-phobes, the ones who can't stand the sight of a single carnation? The Florist shrugs. "It's just like a celebrity who dies, everybody in the world sends flowers, Princess Diana or somebody like that. We had one service where we had twenty arrangements to go to one home, and after about the first ten or twelve, we suggested to the people who were sending them to have us deliver about a week or so later, spread it out a little bit. Most all of them understood and were quite obliging. That way they'll have something to enjoy over a period of time."

After my visit to the Florist, I learned that forty years ago revenue from funeral flowers added up to as much as seventy-five percent of the U.S. floral industry's income, but this has since plummeted to today's puny fourteen percent. What happened? Among other causes, *The American Way of Death*. Jessica Mitford didn't attack just undertakers, she took aim at coffin makers, cemetery owners, memorial manufacturers, and florists. Did her readers realize that flower expenses were averaging $246 per funeral in 1963 (about $1,392 in 2000 dollars)? That florists often used inferior-quality arrangements, which grief-stricken relatives were not likely to notice? That the clergy considered these displays lavish and intemperate, recommending that the money might be better spent on charities (for instance, the church)? That "Please Omit" notices were prohibited in many obituaries because the floral industry blackmailed newspapers by threatening to withdraw advertising?

But mourners haven't given up on funeral flowers, especially in this part of Vermont. "We consider funerals the most important work we do in the shop," the Florist solemnly tells me. "It's a step above weddings, birthdays, anniversaries, everything. We always give priority to funerals. I'll give you an example. Holidays are the worst time to have funerals because we are so busy. One year we had a cooler full of flowers for Valentine's. Then a family came in for a funeral service. I yanked every single flower out of the front cooler, everything we could get. We used the flowers to do the funeral. As far as we were concerned Valentine's was over. There were quite a few disappointed customers, but the family came first."

Flowers and plants weren't always mere symbols of mourning, they once had a practical function. Frankincense and myrrh, those legendary gifts at Christ's birth, also figured in the ingredients for embalming oils used to preserve Egyptian mummies. Could Mary Shelley have had frankincense's death-defying properties in mind when she named *Frankenstein*? Archaeologists have also discovered traces of *Cannabis sativa* and coca plants in ancient Egyptian tombs, presumably intended for the pleasure of the deceased in the Great Beyond. Before refrigeration, fragrant flowers and herbs were used to overpower the stench of decomposing bodies being prepared for burial. In medieval Europe, rosemary was strewn into open graves to sweeten the atmosphere and, perhaps more significantly, the soil, as rosemary raised the pH in what might have been the earliest experiment in biodynamic composting.

The Bible uses flowers as a recurring symbol, referring to lilies, grass, and wheat as metaphors for human life, and admonishing Christians to look to the withering flower's seed as a promise of resurrection. But it wasn't until Victorian England that floral arrangements became the supreme funerary art. Perhaps, like the organ, this change was spurred by fascination with new technology—vast crystal-palace greenhouses that for the first time offered dazzling varieties of exotic species year-round.

Even today, England leads the world in extravagant floral displays, not only for Princess Diana's funeral, as we watched mile after mile of bouquets pile up along the funeral route, but frequently and without fanfare in London's East End. In this working-class neighborhood, coffins are covered with flowers, and so are the hearses. Undertakers must employ additional vehicles to carry the floral overflow on the trip to the graveyard or crematorium. In *Last Rites,* a study of contemporary East End funerals, Glennys Howarth quotes a proud undertaker describing a job for a deceased pub owner.

> We did a publican's funeral recently where there was about eighteen limousines and there was three hearses—(one for the coffin) and the two other hearses were just loaded with flowers. And there was flowers lying on every vehicle and underneath. We just didn't

know what to do with them, you know. And it was just one person and he was a publican. Well known—done the local boys boxing and things like this and just very likeable. That's the way people show their respect, with flowers.

One flamboyant East End funeral provider boasts flower-bedecked, horse-drawn hearses, conveniently rented from film companies, which feature them in period-piece horror pictures. As in so many other "poor" cultures around the world, East Enders lavish a larger proportion of their income on funeral embellishments than the wealthy, as if they know something about death and bereavement the rest of us don't.

With no idea of the floral options available for a funeral, I ask the Florist, who seems surprised at my ignorance. "Most families know what they want when they come in," he says. "Because there's usually somebody in the family who is familiar with funerals, that's been to funerals, ordered flowers for funerals. The hardest ones to work with are the ones who have absolutely no idea what they want. And I don't get people choosing flowers for their own funeral," he says, giving me a curious look. "The way it usually goes, we work with the family or the undertaker. Say a family comes in, normally they make arrangements right here in the shop. Occasionally if they just don't feel like getting out, we will go to the house, or we'll drop off a book showing display examples for them to look through, then we'll take orders after they're done."

He takes a book down off the shelf, opens it up, and I flip through the pages. It's a glossy, color catalog of flower displays arranged rigidly on pallid coffins. The lighting is flat and fluorescent, and the colors, even the reds, look . . . well, embalmed. They remind me of those bleached-out, laminated photos of burgers and fries you see in fast-food windows. The Florist points out different options. There's a heart on a metal stand, baskets of flowers flanking a coffin, a "spray" of flowers on top of another coffin.

"Now if you talk to an undertaker, there are actually two things they use for terminology. Sprays and baskets. And when they refer to baskets they're talking about anything that is on a stand, like a vase or a wicker basket. And when they talk about sprays, it could be a basket spray, it could be your set piece, which is a heart or a pillow or anything that is going to be on an easel." Maybe you won't know your flower types, but you can see whether you want a casket spray, a heart on an easel, or a small satin pillow with a heart to go in the casket. Easel displays are limited to flowers that do well without water—carnations, daisies, chrysanthemums. If you're going to use lilies or iris or tulips or something that doesn't last out of water, then you're going to have to use a saturated-foam-type stand, so they're in water all the time."

I'm beginning to understand why many families suggest "In lieu of . . . ." The Florist mentions silk flowers, which are apparently quite popular with one local family. "They wanted sixty silk roses," he says, "so I did them in two different baskets. Members of the family made themselves a little bouquet out of the baskets after the service was over. Now this one family does it every time they have a burial."

I ask the Florist about using blooming plants, and he tells me they're especially popular at summer funerals, when the family can take them from the church or funeral home to the grave. "Azaleas, cyclamen, geranium planters, they can all go to the burial plot after the service. Blooming plants are also popular for Memorial Day, when people take them to decorate family graves."

Now there's an honest-to-God pagan ritual—Memorial Day, a.k.a. Decoration Day—a gift to us from the Druids, who celebrated the rebirth of summer by dancing around the burying grounds, weeding the graves, and honoring the dead with flowers and plants. The Florist notes my interest in Memorial Day and perks up, admitting that it's a favorite of his. The holiday gives him a chance to get out of the greenhouse, get his hands in the earth. It reminds him of his childhood, working with his grandfather.

"Back when my grandfather was in the business they didn't have all the technology. As far as baskets and vases, the containers were mostly a mâché material, plastics and glassware really hadn't come in yet. They used wire frames, moss wrapped in tissue, stuff like that, for doing their casket covers and casket pieces and sprays." Moss? "Sure, they used moss to do a casket piece, which is designed to go on top of the basket. You had to have the flowers in water somewhat, so they'd soak the moss and tie it with string onto the wire frame and then wrap waxy paper and tissue around it, and then they'd put all their greens and flowers into that. I remember going after the moss with Dad. We had to go down into the swamps looking for sphagnum moss and bring it back home. If you weren't careful you'd get lost."

The Florist reaches up and takes down another book from the shelf. It's a trade catalog of black-and-white photos of floral displays from the 1920s, *Funeral Flowers*. The title is superimposed over a lacy feather. Could be an angel feather, but a raven's would better suit this collection of noir bouquets. The photos are stunning, high-contrast compositions of crucifixes wrapped in lilies, floral hearts on wooden tripods, fireside baskets of carnations. Chiaroscuro high-relief shots grainy enough to give the flowers texture, they remind me of the hand-carved granite roses in Hope Cemetery. How different it would have been to leaf through a book like this with a grieving survivor, when the photos themselves seemed to mourn, before color took the soul out of photography.

Inspired, I ask if he offers black-and-white flowers for the altar. He shakes his head and tells me there's no such thing as a black flower. Too bad. Then he brightens. "Well, sometimes we will spray carnations black for high-school proms, to go with the tuxedo. But people usually want cheerful colors at a funeral." Black spray paint? The fragrance of Rust-oleum drifting through the pews? Interesting concept.

Before I leave, the Florist gives me a tour of the greenhouses. As we walk up and down the aisles of next summer's salads and pumpkin pies, he gets down to the nitty-gritty. "The florist and the undertaker are actu-ally very involved with each other. If they're not, then the florist pays hell. In other words, containers that don't leak. And the arrangements must be done firmly in containers so they don't tip over, they're very stable. All the materials and flowers we use are fresh and don't shatter. We don't want to make a mess in the funeral home. The second problem which has hurt a lot of florists is the quality of flowers. Funerals used to be called 'clean-out-the-cooler time' for a lot of florists, to get rid of old flowers. But we know, the longer they're gonna last, the more pleased the customer is going to be."

Finally, I ask the Florist if working on funerals has affected his attitude toward mortality. "It's made me more aware of death," he nods. "It hasn't made me more callous, but rather more concerned, compassionate about the families. How it can disrupt peoples' lives. I'm a firefighter too, in town, and it's similar. I'm more conscious of people and their problems."

He opens a door to a large storage room. The place looks like it's on fire. The room glows blazing red, the entire floor neatly laid out with row after row of geranium plants in full bloom. The Florist tells me that he'll spend the next few hours in here taking cuttings to propagate new plants, then toss out the old ones. The funeral-flower tradition is all here, the clay pots lined up like gravestones, each new plant a resurrection. You'd have to be a real Scrooge to say, "Please Omit."

THE GRAVEDIGGER stomps on the fresh grave and tramps down the sod, which is cut into neat green squares, like a pan of spinach quiche. A warm May sun filters through the towering Norway spruce trees that surround the cemetery. The branches are heavy with swollen seed cones and nesting songbirds. It's Monday morning, a good day to be on the right side of the grass.

The Gravedigger is starting off the week cleaning up after a couple of weekend funerals. Next to the grave there's a neat pile of dirt that will have to be moved, and a deep tire print in the lawn, a reminder of the backhoe that dug the grave. There was a time the Gravedigger shoveled the holes by hand, until his back gave out and he began calling a contractor with a John Deere. But he fills the graves the traditional way, by hand, and not for sentimental reasons.

"It's the easiest way," he shrugs. "You stand right in there, right on the vault, and pull it in. Doesn't take long." Graveyard traditions may be changing, but sometimes the old methods work best.

I've returned to the town cemetery for a talk with the man who Roto-tills my gardens, teaches my daughter snowboarding at the nearby skiway, fronts an electric blues band, and buries our dead. I wonder what he does on his day off? I hadn't planned on another graveyard visit until one night watching a video of *Hamlet,* when I realized that the only people in the play who weren't depressed, morbidly obsessed, homicidal, or suicidal were Shakespeare's "Jokers"—the gravediggers. Wisecracking, tossing up skulls to make room for Ophelia, posing riddles (including what may be the first theatrical example of gallows humor), they seemed to be the only characters who didn't already belong in a grave. Perhaps the Gravedigger would have something to teach me.

"I got the job from a neighbor," he says matter-of-factly, stomping down on the spongy sod. "She knew the person that was treasurer of the cemetery association back then. She heard that they were looking for someone and I called them up and said, I'm interested. I was originally recruited for maintenance, to cut the grass and keep things up, trim around stones. There's tree work to be done. Brush work. General maintenance, seeding here and there once in a while. And then just naturally since I worked here they asked me if I wanted to do these graves. So it was a good opportunity to make a little extra money. My kids help out sometimes, it gives them a little work, and I'm really grateful for that, too."

The Gravedigger wears mountaineering sunglasses, the kind with the leather blinders on the sides, and a khaki baseball cap with a gray-streaked pony tail dangling out the back. I offer him a doughnut.

"What kind?" he asks suspiciously.

"Plain."

I walk to the car and bring back the box.

"Gotta be careful," he says, taking a doughnut. "I got fat eating doughnuts once. Out to here," he says, holding his hand over an imaginary belly. "I was living on a commune in California. They sold bakery stuff, lots of sweets." He takes a dainty bite out of the doughnut.

I ask him about the job.

"I usually get a call from the treasurer of the cemetery, he's like the go-between between the mortician and me, and I take it from there. I hire out the backhoe, we arrange to meet up here, and I cut the sod out. After the backhoe digs the hole, the mortician's crew makes it nice and neat. They cover up the pile of dirt with this really nice green carpet thing, there's like no *dirt* dirt showing anywhere, no one's stepping in mud or dirt. They like the hole to be about five feet deep, and eight feet long by about forty inches wide. That gives them room to get the vault in there.

I used to always think they buried just coffins, but they have these giant concrete vault-casing things now that the coffin goes in. I guess back in the old days they had to be a lot deeper, at least six feet, to protect against animals going after the body. They had flimsier coffins. Now that they have these vaults, they don't have to be quite as deep." He shakes his head. "It's kind of crazy if you ask me. Why do you want to preserve it? Why not just compost the people? But it's all state law now, I'm pretty sure. You can't just throw a wooden coffin in the ground anymore.

"Anyway, I have to hang around after the service, after the burial, down below somewhere where they can't see me, till it's over, then just come over and do my thing."

"Do you know who you're burying here?" I ask, wondering if there was a death I'd missed, or if it was a body retrieved from the storage vault. A winter death.

"I don't know," the Gravedigger murmurs. "I'm not very good at names. I don't usually pay attention to who it is. It's just a job."

The Gravedigger's instinct to slink away is a common one among funeral workers, a mixture I suspect of discretion and embarrassment at being involved in this dismal business. It's a feeling I've shared during this quest. People look at you differently when they hear what you're involved in. Often, they won't look at you at all.

Historically, gravediggers were usually unskilled manual laborers, poorly paid and, like others in the funeral trade, shunned by the rest of society because of their unsavory association with death. Until recently, they also risked harmful exposure to noxious bacterial emanations from putrefying corpses. In colonial Pennsylvania, schoolmasters earned an extra shilling digging graves inside churches, until the custom was banned because of the foul atmosphere it produced. Church burials were a tradition in Europe for centuries, suggesting that the morbid atmosphere many equate with Christianity may once have been more than simply a mood.

Gravedigging, grunt work though it is, doesn't lack its own peculiar techniques, such as building great bonfires to thaw out frozen ground, and digging holes with stepped sides that support the coffin covers used for repelling animals and preventing the earth from collapsing on rotten coffins. A competent gravedigger had to be able to orient churchyard graves west-to-east to face the risen saviour on Resurrection Day (prohibited for murderers and suicides, who were punished with a north-south plot). Even priests occasionally got into the act, picking up a spade to demark the length and width of a grave in the shape of a cross, and sprinkling the sod with holy water.

I ask the Gravedigger what instructions he received when he signed on, and he laughs. "Well, let's say it was a learning process. They gave me some real broad outlines of what to do. I'd ask here and there, when the mortician and his crew would come I'd ask them, How was the hole? Was it right?" He points across the cemetery. "One of the first ones I did over there, to this day I regret how I did it. Because I was under the impression that some of the graves should have a little lump on top? And that was wrong. Since I did that one, I've meant to flatten it out and of course have never gotten around to it. Every time I go to mow it, it gets scalped."

A couple of thousand miles away in Texas, "folk" graveyards feature intentionally mounded graves, a southwestern style with roots in Africa, Britain, and Native American burial practices. No one knows for sure, but mounding may have been intended to convey the impression of a recent burial, symbolic of the struggle against time's eroding force, or more practically, a method to keep track of the graves. Many Texas graves are also scraped down to bare earth and decorated with stones, shells, toys and furniture. One family member hoeing a grave declared, "Grandpa killed himself keeping the weeds out of his cotton field, and we're not about to let them grow on his grave now." Perhaps the Gravedigger was answering some deep ancestral summons when he mounded up that grave.

"The other thing I've learned," he goes on, "is that it pays to hire a backhoe because if you hit a big rock or some ledge, or some really hard clay, it's too much work to do it by hand. We've had big rocks that the backhoe could barely get out. I had one hole down below, I had to hit it with a pickax, one shovel at a time. Couldn't get a backhoe in there. It was brutal. Thank God I didn't hit rocks, but the clay was enough to just about kill me."

Back breakers like that might have inspired the old churchyard cemetery tradition of recycling bodies, allowing them first to rot, then digging up the bones for the charnel house to make room for more burials. Once you've managed to pry up a graveyard's worth of rocks, imagine the pleasure of being able to use the plots again and again. Records show that over several centuries more than five thousand bodies were buried in a single half-acre English cemetery. The soil nutrients must have been pretty potent.

The Gravedigger has obstacles besides rocks to worry about, such as the concrete that prevents the graves from collapsing. "Sometimes the undertaker will come up here with me, and we'll map out exactly where a grave's gotta be, because with these squares that people buy here, you have to pretty much know where the other vaults are, otherwise you'll dig right into 'em and break 'em. We hit one once and broke the concrete side right off. That's why the undertaker has got this big long rod that he sticks way into the ground to locate what's underneath. Especially with some of the older lots, there's no accurate records about where things are buried, so you have to figure it out. You can pretty much tell when you hit a hollow thing down there, you can tell by the sound when you hit it with that rod. Boom!"

Town gravedigger means being on call seven days a week, the same as his spouse, a midwife, who's bringing people into the world to replace the ones he's ushering out. That makes for shaky family scheduling, especially when he's trying to book a vacation. "There's a commitment there that I can't go out of town, although I did try to hire somebody else to do it for me once. I went out of town, and I hired someone to fill in for me. When they cremate somebody, they put their ashes in a little urn, and you just dig a small hole, a foot and a half deep to put the urn in. Very simple, right? Takes ten minutes. So this friend of mine was going to do the urn thing, fill in the hole. I just assumed everything was going to be fine, it's just like very, very basic. I get back into town and I get a call, all upset, from somebody on the cemetery committee. He said, I went up there and the urn wasn't buried! He didn't put the urn in the hole! And the people were really upset. They went up there and it was just sitting there on the ground. I guess I just assumed that he'd know to put the urn in the ground and bury it. I felt really bad because they got very upset about it, which is understandable, because something like that can open wounds. My lesson was, you've got to be really, really, really thorough when you give instructions to somebody. No matter how stupid it may seem."

Not exactly the enlightenment I was looking for, but I got the message. Again: Plan Ahead. And think of all the time the Gravedigger has for brooding over his own funeral plans. A blues man in a graveyard! The last time I heard him play, the band was set up in a barn for the Fourth of July, and when he started to wail on the harmonica a cloud of bats flew out of the hayloft and the mice came out of the woodwork and ran madly up and down the rafters.

But the Gravedigger shakes his head. "No, I don't think about it that much, where I want to be or where my ashes want to be. I think it's a waste. To go through this whole rigmarole, all this space you use up and everything. This is a waste of land, man! The money they put in just to pay me, it's insane. All this work to trim around every single one of these things. If I had a choice I'd rather be cremated. If I have to be in a cemetery just put me in an urn and a little rock grave."

The Gravedigger shovels some dirt into the tire print and smoothes it over. I'm surprised and disappointed. I was hoping for some wisdom here, straight from the source. A heavy blues chord. You dig graves, you play in a blues band, and you don't think about death? Sure.

"I think I'll leave it up to my kids," he goes on, looking out over the cemetery. "Eventually I'll ask them, would you guys like to have a plot in the cemetery here? So you can come think of me, whatever? If they could care less, I'd say all right, just get me cremated and throw my ashes on the compost pile. My feeling is when you're gone, you're gone. When my grandmother passed away all the relatives showed up from all over the place, and we basically had a big party. I think that's the way it should be, you know? Celebrate the person's life. Rather than just blah, blah, blah. I like the idea of a wild, raucous party when someone passes away. Make it fun." The Gravedigger points out a small headstone with the earth collapsed around it. With Memorial Day coming up fast, he decides to use dirt from the new grave to patch up the old one. When he's finished I ask him about the old traditions, Memorial Day, anniversaries, birthdays. Do people still visit the cemetery to pay their respects?

He nods. "Memorial Day is a big one up here. They all come up. A lot of people make a big deal out of that, they come up and put new flowers on, or plant around the stones." He walks over to an old grave, a tall white marble obelisque on a sturdy pedestal. "Check this one out," he says, kneeling in front of the monument. We take turns teasing the words out of the eroded stone.

"The six children of Royal West . . . a brother of the deceased . . . although benefited thousands of dollars from her estate . . . absolutely refuses to contribute . . . only ten dollars toward the erection of this monument . . . which was regarded with scorn and contempt."

The Gravedigger stands up. "A family feud carved right into the stone, it's pretty rare to see something like that."

Sounds more like a curse to me. I check out the date, 1860, and wonder how the West family has fared since then. Come to think of it, there's no one left in town with that name. Bewitched? I wonder how many families return on Memorial Day more out of superstitious fear than family love, terrified that any sign of neglect will stir up an angry ghost.

The Gravedigger walks down the hill and stops in front of a scruffy pile of dirt and rocks strewn with wreaths of wilted yellow roses. It looks like one of those disaster scenes you see on TV, the aftermath of a terrorist bomb, heaped with flowers.

"O my God," the Gravedigger whispers, taking in the shredded landscape. "This is terrible." He backs up from the fresh grave, horrified. "What a mess. This is like not happening at all. This is pitiful!" The

Gravedigger explains that it was a do-it-yourself burial, which a few families still do.

"You can't mow over this. It's a mess. I don't know how to handle this, I'll have to talk to the committee. Nothing's been seeded or anything!"

I imagine the people who dug this grave, hanging tough until the last moment, lowering the coffin into the hole, when the horror of what they're doing sinks in. They scrape the dirt back into the grave, toss the flowers, and run. What about all that dirt? The hell with it, let's get out of here!

The Gravedigger sighs. "They didn't seed it, there's rocks everywhere. Who's going to pay to fix this? People trying to save money. Somebody dug their own and they left a freaking mess!"

He points out another do-it-yourself job behind us, equally rough, waiting to be cleaned up. But I'd wager these slovenly graves are about more than saving money. The plot alone is close to the price tag for a year's property taxes. Call it tradition, or superstition, but when it comes to dying, some folks need good, old-fashioned, hands-on closure.

THE ABENAKI stands on the parade ground at Fort Ticonderoga reciting textbook lessons to the tourists about the battles fought here, how Indians allied with the French and the British influenced the settlement of North America and the outcome of the Revolutionary War. The tourists are totally transfixed, not so much by the nuts-and-bolts lecture, but by the Indian who looks as if he has shapeshifted out of the eighteenth century in brain-tanned deerskin breechcloth, silver bracelets, earrings, and wampum, with bear grease in his hair and a big green clan turtle tattooed on his arm. Blink and he might disappear.

Since Fort Ticonderoga was opened to tourists in 1909, the Abenaki is the first and only Native American employed to tell the Indian side of the story in a place where natives have lived and died for more than ten thousand years, and where their bones and arrowheads keep popping out of the ground whenever someone tries to pitch a tent or plant an apple tree. At the end of the day he lowers the French, British, and American flags, helps close up the gift shop and lock the gate, and drives back to his cottage on the edge of the fort property. He takes off his moccasins and leggings and medicine bag, puts on a pair of jeans, and goes out for a pizza. He's an Abenaki playing an Abenaki, with one story to tell the tourists and another for his visitor from across the lake.

A friend of mine told me about the Abenaki after he'd visited our town to describe native hunting and fishing traditions as well as Abenaki funeral ceremonies and the reburial of native remains returned from public and private collections. I know something about the Native American Graves Protection and Repatriation Act, how some tribes are burying the remains of their long-deceased ancestors, and I wondered how the rituals are conducted, and what the Indians think about mortality. How do they handle the end of life? I called the Abenaki and we agreed to meet on a Monday afternoon in June. When I looked at the date on the calendar, it turned out to be the Solstice, a sacred day in traditional cultures. At least there'd be plenty of daylight for the drive home.

I drive to the southern shore of Lake Champlain and catch the tiny blue-and-white ferry for Ticonderoga, New York. The lake is narrow here, maybe half a mile across, and I recall stories about how Ethan Allen captured the fort from the British without a single shot, claiming it like an Old Testament prophet, "In the name of the great Jehovah and the Continental Congress." For years, the fortress was viciously contested by French and British troops. On one hot July afternoon in 1758, more than two thousand British troops were slaughtered by the French and Indians. A few unfortunate stragglers were cooked in bubbling cauldrons and eaten by native warriors. To soldiers rowing across this narrow passage, Lake Champlain must have looked like the River Styx.

Ticonderoga has the hangdog atmosphere of towns all across northern New York, over-the-hill places, their streets lined with sad buildings, old people, and a few teenaged mothers pushing baby carriages. Today the flags are all at half-mast, but when I ask no one remembers why. The drought just beginning in Vermont has a firm grip here, and the grass is stunted brown. Several historical markers commemorate Revolutionary battle sites. The only new construction is a black granite memorial to the Veterans of Foreign Wars. It's a ghost town.

I drive through the gates to the fort grounds, down a tunnel of grand shade trees, and everything changes. The grass is green, the grounds immaculate. I pass old iron cannons, historical plaques, and a newer wooden sign prohibiting metal detectors, aimed at artifact thieves. The fort itself stands one hundred feet above the lake, on a bluff near the end of a peninsula overlooking Lake Champlain—a brooding, star-shaped, stone and masonry stronghold that looks like a Dungeons and Dragons castle. Compared to the town, where the present seems dead, the past is here, alive.

The view over the lake is spectacular, wide open, and it's easy to see how this place was once known as the key to the North American continent. It holds a commanding position along the waterway between New York and the north, once the main avenue of commerce, smuggling, and conflict between the British colonies and French Canada. Standing on the breastworks overlooking the lake and forest, I can imagine how this vista looked to natives living here before the white men.

The Abenaki tells me it feels so powerful to him that he chucked a twenty-year career as an auto-body worker, sold his expensive log house in Vermont, and moved across the lake to work as an "Interpreter" for seven bucks an hour.

"After I felt the fort a few times I knew I had to be here," he tells me. "I gave up everything."

We're standing outside his cottage next to a bronze '76 Dodge van that he customized into a rolling diorama covered with his own airbrush renderings of warriors on horseback, spirit eagles, mountains, lakes, dancing Indians, a canoe, and howling wolves. Nearby there's a teepee, and a station wagon with a woodstrip canoe strapped on top, and a black dog on a chain. The Abenaki is getting ready for a big reenactment weekend at the fort, Indians coming in from all over the country. It was a similar reenactment a couple of years ago that first drew him to Fort Ticonderoga. The fort was staging a mock battle, including Indians, who were invited but then told to pay admission. The natives refused to pay, things got ugly, and the Abenaki volunteered as peacemaker. The fee was dropped. Later he was offered a job.

He shows me a photo album of reenactments he's attended, battling colonials in his Indian outfit, standing in a canoe spearing fish with a bow and arrow. I think about the Indians I know, most of them laid-back dudes who settle for pony tails and turquoise and silver, but this guy looks like an extra from *Dances with Wolves*. I can't figure out why a forty-something Indian would be so gung ho. I tried to remember the last time I put on a gray flannel suit and tie and said, Hey, I'm a white guy!

We drive into the village for something to eat. There's a Greek pizza shop that's jungle steamy with a fan as big as a turbo prop blowing hot air around. I hesitate, but the Abenaki walks in. "Doesn't bother me, I stand around naked in the sun all day." We order a pizza, I ask for a beer, he gets a coffee, and we sit down. "I'm an alcoholic," he admits bluntly. "Thirteen years in recovery."

He tells me that he was raised by abusive alcoholic foster parents in Rutland, both dead now of alcoholism. They never told him about his Indian blood. "I was always into strange things that didn't click till way later on," he recalls. "I'd go up into the attic, a dark, dark attic in the summer, and it'd be 110 degrees probably and I'd sit there for hours and sweat. I didn't have any idea why, I would just do it. A couple of times I'd sit in the car and turn the engine on, turn the heater on full blast, see how much I could sweat. And people would say to me, You're a native, aren't you? I thought they meant born and raised in Vermont." He laughs. "And there was my intuition, when I'm hunting—actually knowing when I'm going to see something before I see it."

When he was thirty, he tracked down his biological mother. "She looked at me and said, your father was an Indian, too." By then his biological father had died of alcoholism, and his mother had been in recovery for twenty-seven years. Within a year of discovering his Abenaki roots, he quit drinking cold turkey. "I was just about at the bottom. I know I would have killed myself."

He began developing his native identity, with encouragement from new friends. "I was at an AA dance up at Burlington," he recalls. "There was a young lady there who came over to me and says, You're an Indian, aren't ya? And I says, Well, my father was. She says, Well, what makes you think you're not?"

A few months later she invited him to Grand Isle. He remembers arriving in the van, and she called him to come in. "She was on the phone with the tribal clan mother, very spiritual, so I walk in and the woman on the other end tells this girl, An Indian just walked in and he's a healer, I want you to bring him right up. And I'm thinking, man, that's scary. So she brought me up to Swanton, and upon entering this rickety old house, the old woman came out talking to me, telling me stuff only I knew. I was real scared, she knew everything about me. And it turned out I had, so she said, certain powers. Which I do, only usually I use them against myself. But anyways, she came out with stuff that nobody could possibly know. She gave me my name, Red Hawk." He smiles. "A lot of people at the fort, I tell them and they say, red hot?" He laughs. "And she started showing me different ceremonies, healings, we had a really big connection. She'd lost a son almost fifty years ago on Otter Crick, so when I go fishing on Otter Crick, I talk to him. I give him tobacco and then I call her up and tell her what we talked about. Or I'll be walking through the woods and all of a sudden, Bang—I can't go there. I don't know why I can't go there, I can't go there. Scares me to death. A lot of times those are burials, I find out later."

A woman comes into the pizzeria and recognizes the Abenaki from the fort, and she flirts with him and he likes it. He tells her he just finished shooting a television commercial for the fort, and points to a stack of tourist pamphlets on the counter with his picture on the front. "Five hundred thousand in English, five hundred thousand in French," he says with a grin. After she leaves he tells me that he and his girlfriend split up recently. That's why he's wearing his hair loose, traditional Abenaki style for a single man. "In hopes of finding someone," he smiles.

The pizza comes and we eat silently, listening to the Greek music, feeling the hot breath of the big fan. I think about what he's been through, the legacy of alcohol and abuse and abandonment, the courage it takes to break the cycle, and the power of traditions to give meaning to life. The Abenaki's future is his past. The bear grease keeps him sober.

He takes out a cigarette. "Time for a tobacco ceremony," he laughs.

He lights the cigarette and begins to tell me about Indian reburials. "One came from Turner's Falls, Massachusetts," he says. "Been in a private collection on a farm for three generations. The Abenakis ended up getting that one, and one of the girls called me up and wanted to know where the most western falls on Otter Crick were, that's where she felt they should go. My question was, How do you know it's an Abenaki? There were different tribes fishing there. I think it should go back where it came from. In somebody's farmyard."

The 1991 federal Native American Graves Protection and Repatriation Act directed that Indian remains must be returned from museums and private collections to their tribes. But as the Abenaki points out, who knows whose bones are whose? In a well-documented collection, the identity might be clear. But a skeleton in a farmer's closet? What difference does it really make?

"Their journey's been made," the Abenaki says. "All these people have been dead for two hundred, three hundred, thousands of years. But I also think that as long as they're on earth, and especially if they're on display, I think bad things, and uneasy things, will and can happen. There are spirits. Some people call them ghosts, some people call them souls. Some are more powerful than others. One I knew of, to do it legally, because it was found in New York State, they had to contact the leading Indians that would have been there, the Abenakis of Vermont, the Iroquois of New York, and the Mohicans. All three would be contacted, then it'd be up to one of the three to take over. What's going to be hard is proving whose remains this actually is. They swapped sides of the lake all the time. It's just a law, where the people with remains have to contact all three, then they have to get back in touch and say, Okay, we think it's ours, we'd like it back. Or, Okay, we don't want anything to do with it, we haven't got time. Reburial involves trying to find traditional spots to put them, where they felt the remains would actually be buried originally. Lots of times they were buried with special things. But if not, at least do a traditional burial."

The Abenaki sits up tall and looks out the window. A couple of young blondes walk by and we watch them until they disappear. "Good looking," he grins, and I know we could have gotten up and invited them in. It seems unhealthy to be sitting inside a hot pizza shop on the longest day of the year talking about death. But something has brought us together today, something to be honored.

I ask him about traditional funerals. "Different cultures are different, different tribes are different. Some always did cremations, some just once in a while. I believe there's been cremations done in this area, not all the time, but maybe for certain reasons. I mean we were here for ten thousand years. Personally I've done traditional funerals by lining the hole with birch bark, sprinkling tobacco, putting the remains in, sprinkling more tobacco, sometimes singing, praying. People, if they want to help, can come, take a small shovel with a little dirt, say a prayer and put some dirt on. The two I did were both cremations, but it can be done either way. Actually one old man had a real nice turtle bag, so they had him cremated and put in that bag and we put it in the grave. I don't know if he made the bag to be buried in, but it was a nice one, made out of a turtle shell, leather sewn onto it for a pouch. First thing after he died, I contacted my girlfriend and said, We gotta sing, and we did, right then, for his journey. Now Grandmother Doris would say it was very important to burn cedar and sage, to smudge yourself and smudge the area to be dug. Very important. That's actually to purify you before you start your ceremony. If you want to say any last thing to them, send it with 'em, take a piece of pine bough, say it to the pine bough, silently, and put it in. Kind of a message."

He gets up to refill his coffee and I imagine the old man's turtle-shell bag, and it seems like the most beautiful burial container possible. Natural, durable, poetic. Who more apt than the slow and steady tortoise to carry you over the finish line, to make the amphibious leap from this realm to the next. I vaguely conjure up some story lines for the old man and the turtle: It's his power animal, his clan, his turtle island ancestral roots, his favorite soup. Indian mythology is filled with stories about turtles diving to the bottom of a lake, leading warriors to the next dimension. I've always believed that's been part of my role as a pond designer, creating openings to other worlds. Is this meeting with the Abenaki meant to answer my quest? Is it time for a turtle-shell bag?

The Abenaki sits down again, stares into his coffee, and acknowledges that there have been reburials at the fort itself, remains dug up over the years around the lake and sent to Ticonderoga. Farmers dig something up, someone camping discovers a burial, and they call the police. It might be a homicide. The police take a look, they know the history of native burials in the area, they can see it looks old. From there it's sent to an archaeologist in Pennsylvania for carbon dating, and it turns out to be from 1500. The archaeologist knows it was found in Vermont, so he ships it to Fort Ticonderoga. Before long the fort's rolling in Indian bones.

"The director has been very good about these reburials," the Abenaki assures me. "Very specific as to who he's going to let have the remains, very legal and very respectful. Nobody, nobody sees these reburials. They actually had Abenaki scalps on display at Fort Ti at one time. The minute the new director got started he took everything out of sight. He contacted the three tribes in the area, and now he's waiting for them to decide between themselves who has the responsibility. Until then, nobody sees them, nobody gets them, they're locked in vaults. They're underground in climate control. They won't deteriorate."

Listening to the Abenaki's stories, it's clear that after thousands of years of Indian occupation, a slew of bloody battles in the seventeenth and eighteenth centuries, and decades serving as an ossuary of Indian remains, Fort Ticonderoga is an unofficial charnel house, the peninsula one huge burial mound. Historically, that makes this a remarkable place, but to the Abenaki it means much more.

"There are ghosts all over that fort," he whispers. "There's one military burial of 2,400, from a battle in July, 1758. There's another one down by the old French hospital. Every time they try to plant a tree they find a skull. Hundreds down there. There's the American cemetery, where over a thousand froze to death." He leans closer. "There's ghosts, spirits. One lady works there, she's almost blind, but she tells me, I heard you in the fort last night, I heard your bags tinkling. I told her I wasn't there. But she says she smelled herbs and smudge. People have even taken pictures, and a French soldier appeared when the film was developed. In another picture there was a fire in the fireplace, in the summer! Then about three or four weeks ago, the mason at the fort says to me, I see you this morning. I says, Yeah? He says, You were sneaking up on us. And then we see ya, you run across the field right in front of us. I said, When? He says, this morning. I says, I didn't go there this morning."

Well, I too have seen my share of weirdness. A few years after my father died, we were sprinkling his ashes in the Atlantic, and his spirit made a dramatic appearance. As a blue balloon. But this trip, I wasn't expecting the supernatural. Old myths perhaps, mystical lore passed down from the elders, or burial traditions to appease the legendary spirits. But the man is telling me that it's happening right here, now, all the time. Fort Ticonderoga is a big haunted castle. The dead do not vanish.

The Abenaki finishes his coffee. Then he asks himself the big question. "Why do I want to be there? Why does everybody want to be there, the people working at the fort? Almost every worker there, we get a Friday off and a Monday off, and the day we got off, we're still there. They all come right back. I've even asked 'em, I say, Why? One guy said, I don't know. I've got so much to do at home, but I got up, I just knew I had to go to the fort. Everyone, me included, I don't want to leave. I gotta be there."

He shifts around in his chair, then hunches forward. "What it is, I think, is the thousands that are there. They haven't been forgotten. You take a cemetery, two or three generations and it's just markers there. The original family's not going, nobody's actively going. But last year 106,000 visitors came through the gate here, basically in honor of what happened and those people buried there. Indian, French, British, American, all kinds. But nothing bad happens. The spirits, they're not mad. They're being honored and they know it."

On the way back to the car, the Abenaki buys a newspaper. He holds up the front page. "Fort Ti Gets First Native Interpreter." There he is in wide-angle color, talking to a group of mesmerized tourists. It's an up-beat story about the new guide and interpreter who wears beads and wampum and tells tales about the old days, and about how much the visitors like him, especially the kids. No doubt, he's the major attraction at the fort now. There's nothing about an abused alcoholic discovering his Indian spirit and choosing life instead of death, about coming back from oblivion with a push from the ancestors. Nothing about the spirits that roam the fort. How would you write that tale? It sounds like a crack-pot ghost story, something for the midnight talk-radio fringe. But that's the story I've been looking for since my quest began, an unembarrassed affirmation of the spirit world, without the Astrologer's charts and equivocations. We share a meal, and he opens his heart. A man who doesn't merely bury the dead; he talks with them, and they respond.

I congratulate him on the newspaper story and wish him luck, then catch the last ferry back to Vermont. The lake is like glass; we're the only boat on the water. I watch towering cumulous clouds catch fire as the day comes to an end. The ferry glides through the water, across the clouds.

The sunset is out of this world.

THE BALLOON MAN would have been right at home in the middle of that Fort Ticonderoga sunset, but today there are no passengers on the manifest, so he's earthbound, showing off the latest additions to his Vermont museum. He points out a dingy, gray computer and a bunch of manual typewriters, and a fat, blue, overstuffed couch that had to be lifted to the second floor by airship. The last time I was here he'd managed to collect two dentist's chairs, a barber's chair, a buckboard and a black horsedrawn hearse, an old Bugatti motorcycle, his grandfather's Navy band bass drum, a hovercraft (never flown), a 1950s Flymo lawnmower, and the 1919 Renault that was featured in Lillian Gish's silent classic *Way Down East*. There's also a pair of rubber boots he couldn't bear to throw away, so after he poured the museum foundation three years ago, he filled the boots with concrete and put them on the running board of one of his five fire engines, one of which is a tanker that burned up in a firehouse fire twenty years ago. The museum is also the last stop for hundreds of empty beer bottles swilled at balloon meets around the world, lined up on a shelf above an old hardwood bar. Tucked in with everything else are the hot-air balloons, airships, wicker and nylon flying baskets, and gondolas, including a modified three-wheel Messerschmitt automobile that he occasionally takes flying. Junkyard, gallery, Irish saloon, balloon factory, and museum, the place is a Ray Bradbury fantasy come to life.

The two-story museum is two hundred feet long and forty feet wide.

Instead of using conventional ceiling trusses to hold the building together, the Balloon Man connected the plates with cables bound together with twenty come-along hand winches, which gives the building the strength to shoulder the heavy Vermont snow loads, as well as allowing removal of the cables in summer for large balloon-building projects. The building is stitched together, just like a balloon.

On the upstairs wall there's a thirty-square-foot collage of dog-eared old aerial photographs scavenged from the local dump. It looks like the backdrop for the headquarters scene from *Spitfire*. The Balloon Man winds up the tour in front of the latest addition to the museum, an empty cardboard box that held his mother's ashes. Last year he took off from the grass runway outside the museum and scattered her over the airport. His wife, Louise, was driving the chase car down below. She looked up and saw a swirling cloud of ashes spinning around in a vortex of air. "Up and down, up and down," she mimics the movement with her hand. "Just like an aerial ballet. She loved dance, so it was very fitting."

I've come to the airport to ask the Balloon Man about his experiences with ashes. I liked the Abenaki's account of burying ashes in a turtle-shell bag. It seemed simple and artful and personal. Ashes are so . . . versatile. They can be adapted to all the religion-lite blends of old dogma, New Age occult, Buddhism, alien abduction, cyberspace, and outer space. When Timothy Leary died, he had his ashes blasted into orbit, a good last act for a spaced-out cult hero. Another guy had his ashes packed into a Fourth of July skyrocket and launched at a weekend barbecue. Hard to beat, but this summer a NASA geologist was rocketed right into a lunar crater, where his ashes now mix with moon sand. A lot of folks may have given up on religion, but they sure want to go to heaven.

Wandering around the museum, a surreal sanctuary dedicated to old, discarded, forgotten artifacts, including aviation's oldest flying ships, I can feel my preoccupation with death fading. I feel a comforting kinship with the old Flymo lawnmower, a futuristic rig designed to ride on air and make cutting grass supernatural. It never caught on, there was something harebrained about the idea, yet something fine too. Like many of us. You give it your best shot, along comes the next big thing, and you're history.

I GOT TO KNOW the Balloon Man a few summers ago when I was doing a lot of stunt water-skiing with a friend who had a tournament boat on a nearby lake. The Balloon Man had recently bought the grass-field airport next door, and there were times when we'd be skiing and look up and see a Technicolor rainbow overhead. Had anyone ever water-skied behind a hot-air balloon? Was it possible? A couple of weeks later I got a call. My friend had talked to the Balloon Man, who wanted to try it. He warned us that the wind would have to be perfect, straight out of the west and way over the limit for safe flying. I knew that if we pulled it off, nobody'd believe it without proof, so I got ready to shoot the whole endeavor on video.

One July afternoon with a stiff west wind blowing, we gave it a go. The Balloon Man strapped on a bright yellow life jacket. "All the better to find me," he laughed. Tall and mountain-man bearded, he looked too big for the nylon basket with the word EXPERIMENTAL stenciled on the side. His crew held the balloon down until it was almost bursting with hot air, then let go. The balloon shot up, the wind caught it, and the basket brushed over the treetops and a power line. The Balloon Man released a burst of hot air and began the drop to the water. He was sailing due east at about twenty miles per hour. The skier's girlfriend was driving the boat. I was aboard with the camera.

When the balloon appeared over the trees, the Balloon Man threw a towline over the side. It tangled about half way down. Everybody in the boat swore. The rope was hung up around the handle. The Balloon Man shook the line and somehow it tumbled free. The boat driver slowed down, the balloon closed in, the skier reached up with one hand to grab the handle hanging from the sky, and fell.

The boat spun around. By the time we got the skier up again the balloon was half way down the lake, and we had to chase after it until the skier could grab the rope. This time he let go of the line from the boat, and hung on. After skiing for a moment he began to sink. The Balloon Man hit the burners and with a roar the balloon lifted back into the wind, picked up speed, and the skier took off down the lake.

We watched this fantastic vision sail across the blue mountain water. The driver cut the engine. The only sound was the swish of skis over the water. As the balloon approached the far side of the lake, the Balloon Man released the hot air and the airship ditched in the drink. After we picked them up, I asked the Balloon Man when we'd do it again. He shook his head. "I only do that kind of thing once."

Later I found out that the skier's weight pulled the balloon so far out of plumb that when the pilot hit the burners, the fabric began to melt. As they sailed down the lake the balloon was disintegrating.

A few months later I got a call from the Balloon Man. He'd just finished building a custom-designed basket for another balloonist, and wanted me to shoot a video instruction manual. The basket had some special features for long-distance flying, including a panel that dropped open like a Murphy's bed when the pilot needed to sleep. After I shot the video the Balloon Man offered me a ride.

We took off on a late summer afternoon, straight up into the sunset. The propane burners roared when we needed lift, then cut off. Silence. As we gained altitude, I looked over the hangar roof and saw a large cemetery bordering the airport. I was doing my best to squelch a wave of vertigo and the cemetery didn't help. The Balloon Man must have noticed my fingers clenching the edge of the open basket.

"Don't worry, we haven't put anyone in there yet," he laughed. I looked around as we continued to climb. Mountains, streams, forests, farms, ponds, houses, cars, cattle, roads. And nothing between us and the living map below but a waist-high wicker basket. We were sailing northeast in a light wind at about one thousand feet, skirting the edge of the ski lake. An outboard cut a white wake across the water. A pair of hawks circled nearby, and off to the west the Green Mountains rolled away under another balloon, the sinking orange sun.

I was riding the original flying machine. Fabric, hot air, and no guarantees where you're going to wind up. We flew across the lake, sailed up the Connecticut River Valley, and landed on the edge of a corn field twenty miles north of the airport. A farmer and his family ran out and helped us stow the balloon in the chase van, then invited us onto the porch for strawberry daiquiris. After the second drink they booked a flight to celebrate their wedding anniversary.

AS WE WALK around the museum, I ask the Balloon Man how much of his business is connected to family celebrations. Most, he concedes: weddings, birthdays, engagements, family get-togethers, anniversaries. And funerals?

"You mean sprinklings? Oh sure." The Balloon Man says that he's done several, the first about twenty years ago in Connecticut when he was first learning to fly. "This buddy of mine, who'd gotten married in one of my balloons, had a father, kind of a crotchety guy, and he wanted to share the experience of a balloon ride with the father, thinking this would loosen the guy up a little. He could never quite talk the guy into going, and then finally the old man relented and said, Yeah, I think I'd like to do that! And with that he died! "So my friend called up and said, I'd like to take Dad for a balloon ride. I said, Didn't he die? And he says, Yeah, but I'd like to take him up, in the ash form, and sprinkle him."

Evidently the old fellow, who's name was Hank, had been influential in winning public support for a safety dam in his home town, where there had been a devastating flood. The new dam had done wonders to improve the old guy's image.

"It was his son's idea to take off upwind of the dam and sprinkle Hank over the dam. So we went up there, and this was back in an era when I hadn't a clue as to how to make a balloon really go someplace, the way I do today sometimes. But we figured, Well, we'll head further up the valley, a couple of more miles, and it's all wooded up there. So we found this little clearing and I set up and took off. The balloon followed the valley and there was this ribbon of a river down there, and we went right over the dam and I remember my friend opening up the canister. It was the first time either of us had ever seen a cremated person. We looked at each other like, Wow, that's what it is? And we shrugged and sprinkled Dad over the dam. As soon as we sprinkled him, the freaking balloon turned ninety degrees and just sailed off cross-country! Like it had just done this to get to the dam where he was supposed to be. Because the valley kept going the other way! I remember we both got goose bumps. Woah!"

The Balloon Man's story reminds me that unlike church-sponsored memorial services, homegrown ceremonies tend to have a higher incidence of psychic phenomena. After we scattered my Dad's ashes in the ocean, a blue balloon, kid-size, came rolling down the beach propelled by a stiff tailwind, shot past us, and went bouncing down the sand until it disappeared. None of us doubted that it was somehow a manifestation of Dad's spirit, happily released from confinement. What is it about balloons? You go to the county fair and a kid loses a helium balloon and you can't take your eyes off it as it sails away into, well, you name it. Oblivion? The great beyond?

People who watch the Balloon Man soar overhead make a similar connection. He doesn't advertise his sprinkling services, but they see him up in the heavens, and pretty soon the phone rings. He recalls one family that called, wondering if he could sprinkle their father over his own land. The Balloon Man had to explain that it doesn't work that way, he's at the mercy of the winds. However, he might be able to take off from their land.

"I said, if it was only a quarter-acre or so we'd have to do it real quick!" He laughs. It turned out they had two hundred acres and he thought it could be done. "We went up there and we take off and they had him in two urns and all I thought is, Gee, I don't remember Hank being that big. They were these crockery jobs things with narrow necks, it looked like the Genie could come out of them. I guess they wanted two urns so each could have a souvenir. They started sprinkling, and because of the small neck it was coming out kinda slow, and this couple of hundred acres is getting small. Next thing they pull the cork out of the second one and they sprinkle that and the two of them, the mother and daughter, are trying like mad to get Dad out. It was a riot, bouncing up and down in the basket, the three of us are like, Come on, come on! And my wife could see this from below on the road, a stream of ashes filtering out, and she's thinking, My gosh, how big is this guy? It went on forever! I said, was he a big fellow? And they said, Well, yeah." Since then he advises against narrow-necked urns.

The Balloon Man recalls another flight with a remarkable urn. "When I first got here I'd have flights and go two blocks and wind up in the trailer park. I'd land there and sometimes throw out a line and tether the balloon and take people up and down, and they'd all grin, one or two teeth per person. Everybody all grubby. Anyway, this one morning I land there and people come out of their trailers and I say, Anybody like to go for a real flight? And this family says, Oh wow, our Mom would love to go, she always wanted to do that! So I said, get her out here. Well, she comes out and she's in her bathrobe, and they stick her in the basket, and the way this woman was dressed up was beyond belief! So off we go!" He laughs. "Well, it didn't seem so far after that, but probably another couple of years, her kids called up and said, Mom died and we had her cremated. Any chance we could take her for a balloon ride?" The Balloon Man smiles. "I said, sure, we'll do that. Well, what would that cost? I said it wouldn't cost anything. Oh wow, gosh, you're a good man. So when could we do this? I said, Well, how about this evening? I've got an opening, there's nothing going on." The Balloon Man explains that he doesn't often do sprinklings with other, unrelated passengers aboard because it might upset them. "So they come out and it was like the Beverly Hillbillies, they show up in this pickup truck that's fifteen different colors, fenders tied on and everything, and they've got a couch in the back that half of them are sitting on, and a couple of cases of Budweiser. And they're all going flying!" He laughs. "Well, Mom is entombed in what looks like a granite brick. I thought, Geez, I've never seen a container like that for ashes." He holds his hands about two feet apart. "And this thing, they're carrying it, and it weighs quite a bit. They bring it out of the car and they hand it to each other over the side and they set it on the floor and I'm thinking, Boy, we better not have a brisk landing!" He laughs. "I'm wondering during the flight, how does this thing open up? Must be something on the bottom. We're flying along and at some point I'm starting to announce, Well, we'll be landing in about ten minutes now, and I'm wondering when they're going to sprinkle her. They're not catching my hints, so I say, We're coming up on the Connecticut River, would you like to sprinkle her in Vermont, or in the river? Oh, we're not going to sprinkle her, we just wanted her to go for one more flight!" He shakes his head. "She was embedded in this block, maybe there was no way she would come out, then she was heading home to become . . . a doorstop? Or a jackstand under the pickup truck?"

Some folks just can't let go, even from a thousand feet. Even so, the Balloon Man recommends letting go for the surprising, even mystical rewards. He recalls doing a sprinkling for a family who wanted their mother's ashes scattered over the lake where she'd spent many happy summers at a girl's camp. The Balloon Man had to warn them that he wouldn't be able to go that direction from their place: "You can't get there from here." Instead, he suggested they take off from the shore of the lake itself. "I contacted the director of one of the camps asking for permission, and he said, Sure you can do that, but would you just sort of not really announce the reason for the flight? Some of the girls might freak out!" He laughs. "We took off from the little soccer field, and we kept why we were flying hush-hush. We zigzagged up the lake, they did their little sprinkling, said a little prayer, then we went up Blood Brook Road to land. We came down on this property, this beautiful house, and everybody gets to chatting and it turns out the house had been owned one time by the founder of the woman's camp. It was funny how that fit. It was all linked to the camp. The family thought that was perfect." Scientists would say this was just a windblown coincidence, but when was the last time they went ballooning?

Even a sprinkling by plane can have a feeling of destiny. The Balloon

Man recalls taking one lady's ashes on four balloon flights, hoping to sprinkle her over the family farm, but he never got close. "I called up the daughter who had arranged this and I said, You know, we're not heading that way, I could end up taking Mom on a lot of flights!" He laughs. "So I said, You know, I've got this little tiny airplane, it's a one-seater. Why don't I fly up there and circle the farm then I'll sprinkle her from the open cockpit. She says, Oh great! So I flew up there, and I expected the nucleus of the family was going to be gathered together. But it was just the husband and the dog standing in the yard. To make sure it was the right place I flew a box pattern around it a couple of times. I wiggled the wings and waved, and the guy waved back. I think, okay, this must be it. Then I came swooping in and they had a swimming pool right behind the house, a built-in pool. I'd heard stories of airplane pilots doing the sprinklings, and they open the window and the ashes go out but they get sucked back in! Suddenly they're blinded, they can't see where they're going. So I took this bag and held it behind me as I'm flying, and it's out there and I just inverted it. I quick banked the plane to see how this was going, and she went out as one fell swoop. She hovered as a cloud and the cloud got bigger and thinner then bigger and thinner then settled right into the swimming pool!" He grins, and adds that about a year later he landed a balloon right there. Another coincidence? The same man came out. "I said to the guy, was there a swimming pool here? And he says, Yeah, you're right on it. It was all filled in, and there was grass there. I said, Remember you had your wife sprinkled? I did that from my little airplane. Oh, thank you very much! I didn't say, you know she's right here in the pool! I held back on that. I said, why'd you get rid of the pool? And he said, Oh, my wife really loved the pool, but I didn't like maintaining it, and she was gone, so I felt like I was just keeping it clean for all the neighborhood kids. So I filled it in." The Balloon Man laughs. "I kept thinking, should I tell him that she's in the pool?" He never told, but he seems pleased with how it turned out. The lady's buried in her beloved pool, the husband's free of an unwanted chore, and the Balloon Man, he made it all happen.

I ask the Balloon Man if he ever leads religious services in the basket, like the Navy captain you see reading from the Bible before releasing a dead sailor into the sea. He shakes his head. "No, I'm just the chauffeur." He pauses for a moment. "But you feel incredibly moved by the experience, you get goose-bumpy."

The more stories I hear, the more goose-bumpy I get, too. Like the cemetery alongside, the airport's psychic twin in the body-disposal business. The museum has big picture windows overlooking the cemetery, and last year the Balloon Man came back from a flight and found a note stuck on one of the windows: "View to the Future." A message from the dead, or a joke from one of his customers?

A few years ago he looked out the window and saw a uniformed veteran collecting the small American flags planted on the veteran's graves. He asked what happened to the flags and learned that every year after Veteran's Day they were incinerated in a burn barrel. The VFW burns American flags? Heresy. The Balloon Man offered to gather them up himself, give them to kids on international flights, and sew them on his custom-made baskets. The embarrassed VFW agreed. Now the vets get a final salute in the sky.

I figure that the cemetery is the ultimate spooky synchronicity here, but then the Balloon Man points across the street and tells me about an old house that used to stand there. "Funeral home," he says. "The owner evidently made caskets also. He was the town undertaker."

Not long ago, if you'd told me about a little valley with a big cemetery and an undertaker, I'd see black. But when you add balloons rising into the sky, ashes spinning and swirling, it changes the picture. Ballooning is about going up yonder, bound for glory and not a hole in the ground. Gone with the wind. The funny thing is, I don't think the picture would be complete without the cemetery and the undertaker. My mental landscape is changing.

I realize that my fear has been based on an idea, an abstract intellectual terror, a concept that haunted me because I *thought* about it. I remember what Carlos Castaneda said in the Don Juan books: Never forget that the end is just over your shoulder. I never did. But when death is an abstract idea, it has a disturbing power to become an obsession. It can become an idea that won't leave you alone. But it's altogether different to perceive death as an image. This little valley has allowed me to see death, to visualize it as an image of a propane-powered ascent into Shangri-la, with a cemetery and a lake and an old funeral home, where now and then a balloon fires up and rises spirit-like into the sky. It's too beautiful to be scary! I'm going to try to see this valley whenever death whispers.

When I ask the Balloon Man about his own funeral plans, he surprises me by saying it won't include a balloon flight. "For years I always said when I go I want to be put in some setting out in the woods, leaned up against a tree, just sort of set there with my back against a tree and my legs out in front of me, like I was taking a nap."

That changed when he and his wife had a chance to buy all the stock from a defunct video-rental shop down the road. Balloon rides are slow in the winter, and they don't have a TV antenna, so they figured they'd vegetate for 25 cents a tape. Most of them were junk, but they saved one tape, *Rocket Gibraltar,* the story of an old widower, played by Burt Lancaster, who's on the way out. During a family reunion, he spellbinds his grandchildren with glorious tales of Viking funerals and flaming crematory ships. The kids decide to build him a boat, but when he dies, the adults arrange a conventional funeral. So the kids steal the body, and the old man gets his wish, complete with blazing arrows and a funeral pyre at sea.

"Very moving," the Balloon Man says. "I cried. That's my own vision—building my own Viking boat in advance and having a party out on the lake. Have all these folks show up to shoot the arrows!"

I wonder if the Balloon Man would prefer a Viking funeral over an airborne sprinkling because he can't imagine someone else filling his shoes. Better to retire the number.

A couple of weeks after I talked to the Balloon Man, I took my kids down to the ice-cream stand by the lake. While they were ordering, I heard a racket behind us, and when I turned around, here comes the

Balloon Man driving a Viking ship into the parking lot. He'd taken an old Astro Van, chopped off the top, and built a twenty-foot lapstreak longboat on the chassis. The Balloon Man was driving, and the seats were full of squealing kids. They all jumped out, bought ice cream cones, and drove away.

My own kids were awestruck. "What's that, Daddy?"

I said I wasn't sure, but I thought it might be a Viking funeral ship.

THE CREMATOR waits. He stands in the doorway, a young man wearing faded jeans, a white T-shirt, and latex gloves, and while I'm parking the car I can't help imagining where those pale white gloves have been. I take a deep breath and walk up to the door. He peels off a glove and, what the hell, we shake hands. Then it's downstairs into the flat-roofed concrete warehouse. The room is a big industrial box, white walls and ceiling, gray floor, overhead fluorescents, sparsely furnished with a small desk at one end and a flea-market couch and chairs at the other. Wooden and ceramic urns are displayed on a shoulder-high shelf draped with black cloth that hangs to the floor.

He puts his glove back on and asks me to wait while he deals with a body he just retrieved from the Brattleboro hospital. He rolls back a wide, blue, sliding door and vanishes. For the next few minutes, I look around the room while booming sounds of banging steel echo beyond the slamming door. A couple of generic prints hang on the concrete walls, a goldfinch in a tree, a bouquet of flowers. Several brochures are piled on a shelf, *Cremation Explained, Eco-Friendly Death & Other Choices,* and at the far end a copy of Jessica Mitford's frontal assault on the funeral business, *The American Way of Death.* Not your run-of-the-mill, soft-focus undertaker's sanctuary.

I read about the Cremator a year ago when he made headlines during a fight with the funeral establishment in Vermont. A couple of years out of high school he'd started up a no-frills crematorium in southern

Vermont, offering cremations for a fixed fee of $550, including removal of the body. No hidden costs, no trick contracts. With basic cremations around the state averaging about $1,500, he had the powers-that-be worried, and they pounced. The Cremator hadn't been to mortuary school, they charged: he was unlicensed. Legislators were lobbied to enact a new law requiring that crematorium operators be licensed as funeral directors, a designation that would not only demand an annual fee, but require attendance at mortuary school to learn funeral practices unrelated to cremation.

But the Cremator had no interest in being a funeral director, a vocation he abhors. His ambition was to offer an alternative to the overpriced undertaker, and with some help from the Vermont office of the Funeral and Memorials Societies of America, he fought back. State law, he knew, allowed for the transport of bodies, and crematoriums were already regulated by the Natural Resources Department and the Health Department. He went to the newspapers and they liked the story. It was classic David and Goliath, with David using a cremation oven against Goliath's gold-plated coffins and embalming fluid. The local papers ran with it, then Associated Press, *The Boston Globe,* and National Public Radio. Business took off. The state Attorney General sent him a letter indicating that he had no intention of trying to change the existing law. The Cremator didn't have time to celebrate. He was already flat-out, seven days a week.

I sit on the couch and glance at the yellow Eco-Friendly pamphlet. "Glue is used extensively in the manufacture of plywood and particleboard and, because the glue chemicals would be released in the cremation or decomposition process, caskets made from either are less desirable. . . . The body container that consumes the least of our resources and energy to produce is a *plain wooden box. . . .* Modern cremation units operate with air-scrubbing capabilities to keep air pollution to a minimum . . ." Three cheers for green death.

It feels good to get off my feet. A couple of days ago I twisted my ankle running the chainsaw after Hurricane Floyd flattened a maple tree in the back yard. The rain from the storm was a welcome drought-buster, but it also washed a mouse into the well, and I had to put down a ladder, clean the tiles, flush out the cistern, chlorinate the system, and haul drinking water for two weeks. Meanwhile, both of my kids were sick, school was starting up again, and property taxes were due. Limping up to the front door of the crematorium, the timing felt right.

The blue door rumbles open and the Cremator apologizes for the interruption. A removal planned for last night was delayed because of organ donations, and he stayed up until one in the morning waiting for a call that didn't come until six, but now the body's in the cooler, and we can talk. Only for an hour. There's an undertaker on the way from the Northeast Kingdom to help him make a pickup in New Hampshire, where the law allows only licensed funeral directors to move a body. The professional removal will double the fee, but the Cremator tells me cheerfully that the law will change next year, opening the state to his services.

I ask the Cremator how he got started in this trade, and he tells me he began working for his hometown's cemetery department after finishing high school. Digging graves, taking care of headstones, yard work. "I worked for the sexton who'd been there twenty-one years, and one day he said he wanted to clean gravestones." He gets up, takes a picture off the wall and shows it to me. Two photographs are mounted together, one above the other. Gravestones. The stones on the top are dark, the ones below white. "This is what we do. The top is before and the bottom is after. You know how your car gets oxidation and all that? Well, if you sit out under a pine tree for about 150 years, that's what you'll look like. Dirty, dingy, air pollutants. We do one or two cemeteries a year now." The Cremator tells me that a big reason for the breakdown of the stones is lichen, which is actually eating the outside of the monuments. "We're helping the stones," he says proudly, hanging the picture back on the wall.

A year or so later, he was sitting with his friend in a cemetery one fall afternoon. "I said to the sexton, We've seen so much money wasted and so many people taken advantage of. We'd had a rash of young kids, suicides. Wouldn't it be wonderful if we could do something to help people? My whole ambition was to go outside of the funeral industry and go against the grain. I'd buried so much money in the ground and had seen so many people grieving. I think when people get a bill for seven thousand dollars, or they're told to pay this five-thousand-dollar invoice before they can have a funeral, that's not fair."

A few weeks later he picked up a funeral industry newsletter advertising crematory ovens. One happened to be built in Florida, where he was headed for a vacation with his parents. He met with the manufacturers, and returned home and put together a business plan. The sexton was unable to commit to the new business, so he took out loans, kicked in his own money, and ordered the oven.

I ask the Cremator how he knew he could handle such a gutsy task. Digging graves is one thing, but a crematorium? He tells me that he believes he's been given a special talent for this kind of work. "My entire notification of that was—My boss was on vacation, it was just before Thanksgiving and someone had just passed away. We were sent to the cemetery to dig a grave. Well, we dug down and there was this vault, and it was crushed in the earth. You know, the earth moved. It was a family plot and they were going to bury this guy's wife and he'd been in the ground for twenty-seven years and the vault's all busted so we gotta do something—this isn't good."

What they did was to call the vault company, which agreed to bring over a new vault. The next day he dug a double grave and set in the new vault, with a new coffin inside. In attendance were the undertaker, his assistant, two men from the vault company, the backhoe operator, and the town manager.

"Nobody really wanted to get in the hole," the Cremator says. "Well, me and the vault guy said, Give us the gloves, we'll get down and do it. Didn't bother us. We put our masks on. We were going to put straps underneath, kind of hoist the body over. Well, I reached down with a strap, trying to put it underneath. God, this leg feels too solid! I'm trying to pick it up and the guy's got a prosthesis on! From the knee down." The

Cremator whistles. "So we're starting a jigsaw puzzle. I put the first piece of leg over in the casket, and everybody's around the hole watching me and this gentleman."

"This is an embalmed body you're dealing with?" I ask.

"Oh, yeah, but of course after twenty-seven years all it is, pretty much, is a brown leathery skin consistency, and the clothes. There was also water in there because it was crushed. So I reach down again and grab another, gonna put the strap under, and by God there's another prosthesis leg, he had two, he was cut off at the knees. We couldn't figure out why he had all these canes in the casket."

I wonder if his relatives included the canes so he'd have them up in heaven, although on the other hand you'd hope that by then he wouldn't need them.

"Some of the people who were watching, they couldn't eat all day long after that," he continues. "And I wasn't really affected. It didn't bother me. So from there on out, I knew I had an ability. Things kind of got rolling along after that."

The Cremator stands up and offers me a tour of the place. He rolls back the blue door and we step into the crematorium room. The roaring oven fills most of the space. It's a hulking, green, rectangular, steel structure that looks like a maple-syrup evaporator, with a big steel chimney rising from the back. There's a digital dashboard on the front of the oven, and a gauge with red numbers flashing out the temperature: 1,600 degrees.

He leads me past the oven, opens another door, and we step into a larger room, unpainted, with his van parked just inside a large garage door. The place is pretty much vacant, except for a box sitting beside the entry, draped with a green cloth. He lifts the cloth, revealing a plain pine coffin with mortised corner joints. The Cremator tells me he's storing it for the gentleman who made it, until the day it's needed.

"You're keeping it for him?"

He nods.

"No charge?"

"No."

Nice. The builder satisfies the coffin building urge, then gets the thing out of the house. That's peace of mind.

The Cremator tells me he's renting the warehouse from a Fortune 500 firm with a lot of different companies. They don't need the space.

"Know what they used to make here?" he asks.

I shake my head.

"Coffin covers."

WE'RE BACK in the waiting room and the Cremator is telling me why the business is successful. "People want to have an alternative," he says. "They don't want to spend their life's fortune." He stands up. "Now, funeral directors, they're kind of slimy." He mimics a conniving undertaker. "They come up to you and they put their arm around you and a little fake tear comes out of their eye, and they reach in your back pocket . . ." He pulls out his wallet and tosses it across the room. "And there's the assistant dumping out all the money!" He strides across the floor, scoops up the wallet, and fishes out the bills. He hams it up like a silent-movie villain. "Sure, that's a cartoon and it shouldn't be like that, but it is, really. They are there telling you that you need all this stuff and you need this casket, and this, and this, and this, and the profit margin is so disgusting. Say you bought something for $50 and you turned around and sold it to the public for $1,100. Is that white collar crime? They all go to mortuary school, they learn the same trade. How to feed off your inability or vulnerability because you're emotional."

He sits down and looks me in the eye. "You can celebrate a person's life whether you spend one dollar or one million dollars. What I'm helping people do is take care of their own, giving them back their original rights. Because here, you have many different options. You can have me do the removal, and all the paperwork, and kind of take your hand and walk you through the whole process. Or some people—it's rare, maybe ten percent—do their own."

In Vermont, the Cremator tells me, there's no requirement to remove a body from the home for up to three days, and he knows some families who have their own vigils. "You don't need embalming and stuff like that. They dress 'em up and put makeup on and oils or whatever, and flowers, lay them inside the pine box and sing and laugh and cry. That's what it's all about."

The more the Cremator tells me, the more I understand that this is a man with a calling. How else to justify the rental payments, the $100,000 loan, the money he mustered up on his own, the answering service, the warehouse paint job (140 gallons), the nonstop traveling, the propane bills (40 to 80 gallons per cremation). He even builds a pine box for each cremation. No wonder he's working seven-day weeks. But at $550 a head, can he make a living?

"I make a good fair day's pay," he says with pride. "I just bought a house this year. I'm the kind of guy that doesn't need a million dollars in my pocket. I just need to be able to have food on the table, a roof over my head, and some fun. You don't need a lot of money to have fun if you've got an imagination." The real bottom line, he says, is helping people get through a rough time.

He tells me about a man who died at home not long ago. "He hemorrhaged about three pints of blood on the floor of his house, and I went in and cleaned it all up for the family. The guy had lung cancer and he just . . ." He snaps his fingers. "Blood everywhere. This was an old house, and he was a big man, 250 pounds. Thank God the ambulance crew was there because I couldn't get my gurney upstairs, it was a bunch of right angles. So they brought their backboard in, it was me and the police officer and two ambulance workers, and we put him in a body bag and got him into my van. The wife didn't want to be there, she went down the road and stayed with some friends while we were taking care of all this. I went out to my car and put on my protective clothing and I went upstairs. I asked for some warm water, and of course I carry supplies with me, some Envirocide, stuff that's gonna kill any disease in the room. And I took all the bloodstained everything to be cremated with him. They told me that probably no other funeral director would have done that."

The Cremator yawns and stretches. "I had a situation, an old bus driver who I knew my entire life, and he died in my hometown. His home was an old farmhouse, and I had to pick him up in my arms and carry him down a flight of stairs. Those are the things that a lot of people can't do."

That's it, of course. Most people can't hack death. So we have funeral directors, coffin makers, gravediggers. Once upon a time, no doubt, more of us could handle the process. Perhaps it was indifference. After a few plagues, why get worked up about one more corpse? But now we pay an army of health professionals to keep us going twice as long as we did a century ago, and death is twice as scary. That makes death workers more like aliens with supernatural powers. How do they do it?

The Cremator tells me it's a gift. "I know God, and I believe this is what I was meant to do. What I'm doing is probably part of God's work. I was put here to help these people get to the next stage of life, which is hopefully heaven or whatever's next. And if there is nothing beyond life here on earth, that means we better make the best of everyday, and enjoy everything that we're here for. It isn't about the money. If it was about the money I wouldn't be doing it for $550 dollars. People told me I was crazy, that was a ludicrous number—how did you come up with that? I said, As long as I can pay my bills I don't think it's a lot of your worry."

The Cremator gets up, steps into the next room, and returns with a gray container in his hands. He hands it to me. It's heavy, about a foot and a half long, six inches square, with a removable top. It has a greasy soapstone texture, but he informs me that it's a composite made of granite dust and glue. It is, of course, an urn, which the Cremator says he includes in the cremation package, along with a plastic scattering box, giving his customers the option of burying the ashes, or scattering them, or some of both.

He shows me a form his customers can fill out, which amounts to a Statement of Funeral Wishes, a formally witnessed request for his services. The form states that the Cremator will transport the decedent to the crematorium (up to a limit of three hundred miles); complete and file proper authorization forms, permits, and medical examiner's permit; complete the cremation; and supply a scattering container and urn (customer's choice of gray, brown, or blue). He refuses prepayments, steering clear of the potential for preneed fraud. "If you want to put some money aside, put it in the bank."

It occurs to me to sign right now and end my search. I've seen enough, heard enough stories, and death is getting old. Maybe that is what's behind the look you see in undertakers' eyes, waiting at the back of the chapel, for the service to end. It's not the look of a vampire so much as the expression of someone who's seen it all a thousand times, knows he'll see it again, so what's for lunch?

Why not sign? I like the Cremator, and I like the idea of supporting a local maverick whose idea of success isn't just the bottom line. He reminds me of myself when I moved to Vermont thirty years ago, looking for a way to build another culture, but I did it by homesteading, building ponds, writing books. The Cremator is working on a way to take one of life's primary rites away from the tyranny of the undertakers. It's enough to give you hope for the next generation.

How about one more look before I go, just to be sure? The blue door rumbles open and we enter the room. The oven is roaring, and he has to holler to be heard over the thunder of the propane burners and the fans. "The cremation oven runs on a multi-chambered setup," he shouts, pointing toward the back of the pounding furnace. "The first chamber in the back is set to preheat to 1,600 degrees Fahrenheit."

He opens a metal peephole and I look inside. There's a volcanic orange fireball in there, fed by a flame shooting in from a hole in the rear wall. It looks like the shuttle blasting off. Near the window I see a rib cage enveloped by flames, and closer still, the top of a skull.

"The body is in the main temperature-control area, it's called the cremation chamber. You hear the air blowing? Air is pushed in here. There's a burner right here in front and once it's preheated, it ignites the body and the air pushes the fire all around. To look at the beginning of a cremation is like looking into the sun!"

The Cremator says that the body is almost done, which looks like an understatement to me. Well done, at least. Since bone does not decompose, what's left will be skeletal remains, a brittle, glass-like material. I close the peephole and he shows me a steel pan and several long brooms he uses to clean up the bones.

"We let the machine cool down and put on all the safety devices and reach inside with the brooms and sweep everything out, then you get inside with the shop vac and vacuum everything out."

He swings around to a metal countertop and shows me a big gray magnet he uses to remove medical devices from the remains, excluding pacemakers, which must be removed prior to cremation because they tend to explode. He picks up a metal spike from a coffee can and holds it in his palm. "Hip pin," he explains. The magnet doubles as a hammer to smash up the bones, which are then put in a grinder. "And then all you have left is particle matter, there's no visible bone, it's all ashes. We put the ashes in a temporary container, put all the paperwork together, and return you to the family."

You? Did I hear that correctly?

The Cremator spies a fragment of bone on the countertop and smashes it with the magnet. "A little bone left over from someone." He smiles, picking up the ashes and letting them sift through his fingers, like grains of sand in an hourglass.

"That's it?"

"No, I hand-deliver everybody home."

"You get them and then you take them home?"

He nods. "I've only mailed two people. One was to Alaska, and one was to Pennsylvania. Everybody else went home in my arms. I brought them here, I'll bring them home."

Before I go, he shows me his hearse, an unmarked white Caravan, not a hint of black anywhere. He slides open the door and I see that the back seats have been removed and replaced with a four-wheeled aluminum gurney. I catch a whiff of that sour chemical smell I've encountered in funeral homes, medical school dissecting labs, and morgues. The Cremator closes the door and tells me about his first hearse. He built hot rods in high school, and his favorite was a '59 Chevy Biscayne. "It was a pan-elled sedan delivery wagon. It had a big motor and we customized it. Siamese taillights, coffin rollers in the back." A hot-rod hearse.

I ask if that first hearse started him down the road to the funeral business. He shakes his head. "No, I've always had a fascination with the afterlife. I've always been comfortable with death. Ever since I've been old enough to think, it never bothered me. My Mom is a hairdresser, and the funeral home in town used to call her up to go down and do one of her client's hair." He smiles. "I grew up in a family where everybody's always open and honest, talking about everything, feel the way you feel. My parents back me one hundred percent. And my girlfriend rides with me, she'll help me do a removal."

The door opens and an older man in a black suit and tie walks in. It's the undertaker from up north, ready for the removal in New Hampshire. The Cremator introduces us. The undertaker stands motionless, ever patient, waiting. But he seems uneasy, out of place in this funky ware-house, as if the atmosphere might be contagious. Planning their trip, the men stand beside the cemetery photos. Young and old, light and dark, the men mirror the before and after gravestones on the wall. The under-taker stiff and unsmiling, a soldier in the old guard, and the high school hot-rodder, born, it seems, to shake up the death trade.

HALFWAY HOME I remember the request form. I pull off the Inter-state at the next exit, find a Quick Stop and buy a beer. The hardest part of this whole thing is giving up the attachment to my body. Making plans to drop my corpse in a hole in the ground or incinerate it in an oven feels like treason. Maybe I should think of it as if I'm being . . . fired. But it's a job I hate to lose. I sign the form and drink a toast, looking out at the Green Mountains. The leaves are starting to turn. I start the car and head home with the cold beer between my legs, the mountains just roll-ing by, and Steely Dan rocking us down the road. *Those days are gone forever, over a long time ago . . .*

THE GRANDSON is a handsome old-timer with ash gray hair, an easy smile, and a thick Yankee accent. He lives in a small ranch house along the highway leading into Groveton, New Hampshire, where he spent forty years pulping softwood in the mill, and now at seventy-seven he's retired, taking care of his wife, who's recovering from a stroke.

The front lawn is neatly trimmed. There's a new, green Blazer in the garage and a faded, red Toyota jeep and a pontoon boat in the yard. It's been sixty years since he moved across the river from his hometown in Guildhall, where the jobs had dried up after the log runs on the Connecticut ended, but his ties to Vermont are strong. He's got a camp on Maidstone Lake, and lots of kin in Guildhall, most of them in the Pleasant View Cemetery. One of them is George "Ginseng" Willard, his grandfather.

It's a fine day for a trip to the Northeast Kingdom. Driving north on the Interstate, the trees cycled deeper into fall, shifting from lemon yellow to orange and bronze and blood red. The morning sun warmed the hills and the cobalt sky filled with migrating hawks riding invisible thermals. Flocks of hungry ravens circled over the granite ledges. Along the state road north of St. Johnsbury, porches were decked out with jack-o'-lanterns and dried corn stalks and faceless ghosts made out of old bedsheets. I passed a pine tree with a witch plastered to the trunk, impaled on her own broomstick. Farther along, another black-caped spirit was flattened against the wall of a house. New Age white-witch feminists have their work cut out for them here. In the Kingdom, people take their ghosts seriously, and Salem doesn't seem all that long ago.

Crossing the bridge into New Hampshire, a Mack truck dealer displays the biggest American flag I've ever seen. The stiff wind shaking my car barely ruffles the flag. A few fat cumulous clouds cast huge shadows on the White Mountains, like dark rolling lakes. Everything up here moves in slow motion.

The Grandson introduces me to his wife, who's watching a soap in the living room. The room is crammed with easy chairs and an overstuffed couch. The walls are covered with family pictures and souvenir-shop knickknacks. A green Christmas ball dangles at the end of a light cord. It's warm and cozy, but I'm not sure Ginseng would have been comfortable here. I ask the Grandson to tell me what he remembers about his grandfather.

George, as he calls him, lived alone in a cabin just off the main road, where he moved after he split up with his wife. "I was down there a lot," he says. "He'd tell us stories, evenings by the fire, all about the woods and digging his ginseng, getting porcupines and cutting the toenails for necklaces. You know what he used to do?"

I shake my head.

"Cut them pine knots and put them in the fire. He liked to hear 'em snap." He laughs.

He remembers his grandfather's pistol, a Colt .45 with steerheads on the handle, and also the "Bobcat," the dance hall the old man built with the only hardwood floor in the north country. "We used to go down there, and we had roller skates, and he'd let us go in there and roller skate. Beautiful floor."

In addition to collecting and selling ginseng, the Grandson recalls how the old man made spruce gum. "He'd have a wood-fired steamer there and he'd put fir boughs in it and that gum he'd chip off the spruce trees, and then he'd make little sticks there and sell it in his store."

"He had a store?"

"A small one."

He says he has something to show me and gets up, and when he returns he's carrying a faded gray book with black letters on the cover. CASH. He opens it and flips through the lined pages. "This is one of those old books, it's made out of rag paper."

I leaf through a few pages filled with pencilled signatures. "Everybody came through would sign that," he says. He shows me a page with "1931" neatly inscribed at the top. I do a little calculating. There was a killer depression going on, and perhaps even worse, Prohibition. "Look down through here, see this name here?" He points out a signature halfway down the right page.

In a small pencilled script I read, *Henry Ford, Detroit, Michigan. September 19.*

"Henry Ford? What's he doing here?" I look at the next signature, same day, directly below Henry Ford. *T. A. Edison, New Jersey.* Thomas Alva? I recall that Ford and Edison were good friends and traveling buddies. In 1931 they would have been a couple of elderly tycoons on a jaunt to the north woods to check out the autumn foliage, and maybe more.

"What are these guys up to?" I ask.

"They'd hear about him," the Grandson says with pride. "They came from all over, Boston, New York, everywhere."

"Katherine Hepburn's in there," his wife adds smiling.

I check out the pages, and while most of the addresses are local, here and there I find Florida, Washington, New York. Next to a Hollywood, California, address I find *Robert Armstrong* in a confident hand. Star of *King Kong, Mighty Joe Young, G-Men,* and a dozen other romantic thrillers.

Indeed, the Northeast Kingdom was a popular place for tourists who came north to soak up the fall colors and, during Prohibition, Canadian whiskey. They traveled by rail and stayed in grand resorts on both sides of the river. But Ford and Edison, Hepburn and Armstrong, weren't your ordinary leaf peepers. Perhaps they were looking for something more than maple leaves and booze. Just north of Guildhall is Brunswick Springs, the legendary mineral springs known for five varieties of therapeutic—some say supernatural—waters. For centuries Abenaki Indians had used the springs for healing, and after applying the waters to cure a badly wounded British soldier during the Revolutionary War, word of the site's power spread. The Indians warned the settlers not to use the waters for profit, but the temptation was too strong. Since the mid-nineteenth century, three resort hotels have been built there. They've all burned.

The last of the three hotels to go up in smoke was destroyed in the spring of 1931, five months before Ford and Edison's visit. It's possible they had been scheduled to visit there, perhaps even sampled the waters despite the fire, which never halted the springs. The last time I visited, an iron stairway that survived the fire led me to the flowing waters.

And then there was George "Ginseng" Willard, dispensing his own herbal fountain of youth just a few miles down the road. Ginseng, "the sacred man root," is revered around the world as an all-purpose panacea, blood cleanser, energy booster, and aphrodisiac. The Asian variety, *Panax ginseng*, has been prized in China and Japan for centuries, and the North American variety, *Panax quinquefolious*, was well known to Native Americans. When Jesuit priests introduced the American variety to China in the nineteenth century, it became so popular that many New England farmers could make more money harvesting and exporting wild ginseng than growing crops. It's never been as popular here as in Asia, but American ginseng was used extensively in patent medicines during the late nineteenth century, and has long been prized by natural healers and herbalists. Who knows how much of the sacred root those tycoons and movie stars used? Perhaps we have Ginseng and his roots to thank for the Model T, the electric light, and *King Kong*.

I flip through a few more pages and suddenly the signatures stop and the pages fill with erratic pencilled scratchings, jagged as cracked ice. I read the entries aloud, slowly, translating Ginseng's entries. "Why did they nail the manger boy to the cross? Because they were afraid that he was going to be the boss. . . . Men and women are the direct cause for all the sufferings and misery that has come into the world. . . . Sometimes I am sad and sometimes I am glad but there are more times that I am sad than there is that I am glad."

"He sounds depressed," I suggest.

"He used to say we're like the clouds," the Grandson's wife remembers. "Here today and gone tomorrow."

I read another entry. "If hopes had never been born they never would have been blasted." I imagine an old man alone in his cabin with nothing to look forward to but death. No wonder he built a coffin. I turn the page and find several pages have been ripped out. I ask them what's missing.

"I know what happened," the Grandson says. "He wrote some stuff about his wife in there and my mother tore it out." He laughs.

He's talking about Ginseng's daughter defending her mother's memory. Understandable no doubt, but Ginseng got the last word. The winter Bob Pike visited him, a few years before Ginseng died, the old man gave him this account of the marriage.

> I got married when I was twenty-two years old. We lived together five years and then we decided to split muskrat skins. You see, I'd been working in the woods one winter, and I came home and found her living with another man. It annoyed me so I went down to Lancaster and bought a revolver, intending to shoot him, but I waited to get my hair cut, and when I'd got that out of my eyes, it seemed as if I could see clearer, and I said to myself, "George, it's more of a punishment for him to have to live with a woman like her than it would be if you killed him," so I let him go. I guess he was sorry more than once I didn't shoot him.

THAT STORY captures Ginseng's ornery charm, the shrewd yarn-spinning jokester, the "greatest example of God's carelessness in the north woods," as Pike put it. That's the Ginseng I admire. But these sad scratchings show the dark side of the loner existence.

"What a life it is to live where hearts are always sad and never glad. . . . The worst company that a man can get into is his own company. Evil thoughts will come. The only way he can get rid of them is if he is to say, as the manger boy did, get behind me, Satan. . . . How I shall miss the beautiful fires that I have in my camp when I come to lay beneath the clay."

I turn the page. The rest of the pages are ripped out. "Well, at least he got buried in his coffin."

"No, no he didn't," the Grandson says. "My mother wouldn't allow it. She said, He ain't gonna be buried in that!" He laughs.

I'm stunned. They didn't use the old man's homemade coffin? After all the carpentry, the plans, and showing it off in a book? And then suddenly I'm laughing, too. He tears the rosewood piano apart, puts together his last overcoat, even sleeps in the damn thing, and they stick him in a store-bought box! The Grandson and the wife and I are all laughing, and I hear the Undertaker's words echoing in my head. *Funerals are for the living.* I see the three of us, all of us, each with our own infirmities, all headed for the same place, and it's just fine. A mountain of weight lifts off my shoulders. The weight of a coffin.

"You want a glass of water?" the Grandson asks. "Spring water from Vermont."

I nod. "That would be great."

THE GRANDSON turns the Blazer around on the lawn and we roll out onto the highway and cross the bridge into Vermont. When I mentioned that I couldn't find Ginseng's gravestone last winter, he offered to take me to Ridgewell Cemetery and show me. First we swing onto a gravel road and he shows me where Ginseng lived. Gone are the dance hall, the store, the cabin. A camper belonging to Ginseng's great-grandson sits parked on a small field enclosed by pine trees.

We drive along the road and he points out the two farms Ginseng bought but never lived in, and a pond he dug and stocked with trout. Hanging on the front wall of the first farmhouse is a big white sheet with a message painted in black. WELCOME TO VERMONT THE NEW COMMUNIST STATE. A long noose dangles from the eaves.

"My brother lives there," the Grandson says. "He's had some trouble with the state." He tells me that his brother owns a bunch of land in Vermont, so I suppose it has something to do with state environmental laws impinging on landowner's rights. Recently there was a big buy out of timberland by the Nature Conservancy, and the loggers are pissed. So the old timer lives on.

The road passes another farmhouse, where the Grandson was born and raised. We climb past a few hunting camps, past a rusty old school-bus with a smoking chimney poking through the roof, past the sugarbush where Ginseng dug the precious roots, then back to the main road and the cemetery.

The cemetery is laid out on secluded river-valley moraine with spectacular mountain views and a small dairy farm across the fence. Painted big and bright on the barn wall facing the cemetery is a red and blue hex sign. The sun is warm and easy, and many of the gravestones are decorated with flowers and American flags. Off in one corner of the cemetery a maintenance man landscapes a fresh grave. We walk between the stones and the Grandson points out the graves of several cousins and two brothers, then he stops in the shadow of a cedar tree and kneels down beside a depression in the grass. I watch him rake back the undergrowth with his fingers and tear out a few clumps of moss around the edges of a flat stone marker. The stone is about sixteen inches by six inches, not much bigger than a license plate, and it's flecked with pale green lichen. The Grandson dusts off the stone and I read the inscription. WILLARD.

"This is it?"

He nods.

The lettering reminds me of those Gothic typefaces you see at the close of an old black-and-white film. THE END. I kneel down and help the Grandson weed the edges of the stone until it's cleaned up. He doesn't like the look of the sagging stone, and tells me he'll be coming back to jack up the marker and shovel some gravel underneath. We stand up again and he points out a red granite headstone standing about ten feet east.

"That's my grandmother and her second husband," he says.

What would Ginseng think about being buried in the shadow of his ex-wife's grave, not to mention her second husband? One more betrayal, or just another cosmic hoax? A raven cackles from the other side of the cemetery, then lifts from a tree and flaps away toward the Connecticut River, looking just like a witch.

I take a small paper bag out of my pocket. Before driving north this morning I looked through the cupboard hoping I hadn't thrown the stuff out. A couple of years ago, just after my divorce, I bought some ginseng tea. Someone said it was good for depression. The brew tasted God-awful, and I never tried it again. Later I asked an experienced herbalist what she thought of the sacred man root, and she told me it was a "very strong herb," best suited for people sixty or older, especially those recovering from an illness. "But for most of us it's like putting jet fuel in a VW," she cautioned. "It's popular in our culture because we want people, who are designed to go 50 miles per hour, to run at 120. It's good at jacking up your metabolism. There's a huge energy rush. But it can burn out your engine." A couple of books on ginseng and natural healing confirmed her remarks. The herb has potential as a healing agent, but the side effects can be nasty. Small, limited-duration doses are recommended. Most startling was this caveat: *American ginseng is not the best choice for people who are elderly, run down, or fatigued.* The author warns that ginseng can be harmful to people with high blood pressure, diabetes, and low white-blood counts. It's a nervous system depressant.

I wonder if Ginseng's black moods were fed by the wild roots he chewed on. The fountain of youth turns out to be toxic. An old story, really. Mother Nature doesn't intend for us to live forever.

I tear open the tea bag and scatter the ginseng powder on the gravestone. A small dose, just for old times' sake. I try to think of something to say, but my mind is blank. I decide to simply listen.

Silence. Beautiful silence.

I thought I'd come here to wish Ginseng goodbye, but it's more like hello.

THE WOOD TURNER hollers from the yard in front of his tarpapered workshop. "Bring the victim in!" he commands with mock Gothic menace, and for a moment I wonder if he's talking about me or the chunk of maple I'm carrying. Then he laughs, a burly, bearded Grizzly Adams time-warped into a New Hampshire suburb, and I shoulder the maple log up the path, dodging six-foot butt logs, engine parts, and metal scraps surely piled high enough to piss off the neighbors here in the richest college town in northern New England. His place is a rickety monument to the pioneer families that logged and farmed the New England wilderness, who wouldn't budge when Horace Greeley said go west, the last hold-out against sheetrock and satellite dishes. It's no small irony that his fussy neighbors line up to pay three or four hundred a crack for his bird's-eye-maple salad bowls and handcarved men in the moon. I hear he's got the only lathe in the north that can turn a maple limb into a funeral urn.

I follow the Wood Turner into the workshop, down a narrow sawdust trail between electric lathes, chisels, sharpening wheels, crates and boxes and barrels, until he stops in front of a sawdust pile. He sweeps it away to reveal a pink and gray pattern lathe. "The Studebaker memorial lathe," he announces. "Same colors as Dad's old sedan." I hand over the chunk of maple and he mounts it on the lathe.

Chainsawed out of the field, the wood looks too primitive for even this old machine. The bark is reptilian and encrusted with moss and lichen. It's just a piece of green limb wood, after all, the remains of a towering maple that split and crashed after a midnight assault by Hurricane Floyd in September. But it's part of my life, an honest-to-God family tree. Over the past twenty-five years I've watched that maple plow through the seasons like a windjammer, raising green sails in the spring and reefing them in ahead of the winter winds. We tapped it and boiled the sap into maple syrup for pancakes and sap beer, hung a tire swing on a branch for the kids, and buried dead cats under the roots to be taken up and reanimated, praying that's the way it works. Sometimes in the dead of night I hear them, like wind screeching through the branches. When the tree went down a part of me went with it. Bucking up one of the limbs for firewood, I knew I'd found a container for my ashes.

I BEGAN THIS journey with the notion of building my own coffin, hoping that in the process I'd come to terms with mortality. I was inspired by George "Ginseng" Willard, a Vermont logger who'd built his own rosewood coffin and posed beside it for a photographer looking flinty and brave. But I found there was more to death than coffins. There were cemeteries to consider, and gravestones, body donations, and wills. I began to wonder how much coffins matter. It was the people who fascinated me, an underground culture of funeral workers, shunned by the mainstream. They had an intimacy with death, an honesty about fate I'd never encountered before. The longer I spent in the underground, the more clearly I saw the real challenge. As the Stone Carver said, the hard part's not the dying, it's the living. The fear of death I was hoping to overcome was part of a larger fear that had crept up on me, a fear of life. It was the weight of fifty years of hard living, booze, divorce, and dreams that would never come true.

I had no idea where my pilgrimage would lead, or if I'd survive it. But I knew I hadn't felt so alive in years, making my funeral plans. It was a journey with some of the death-defying thrills I'd found before, riding motorcycles, sky diving, and water-ski jumping. There were graveyards, funerary showrooms, morgues, and crematoriums. At first I was fearful, dreading the visits as much as the open door on my first jump plane. I remember a moment of panic talking to an undertaker in a basement showroom, appalled at the chemical smell, astonished that anyone could spend a lifetime here, or even a minute. Yet a few months later I was able to walk into a morgue, look at my first dead body, and not feel like running. When I began I'd lost my nerve, and now I had it back. I was ready to think about living again. There was just one more chore.

I didn't want a coffin. What's the point, if you're not headed for the graveyard, where mandatory concrete vaults seal you off from the earth forever? Besides, look what happened to Ginseng. His last overcoat turned into a straitjacket. Who can blame his daughter for not burying him in it? Imagine being compelled to listen to your father's homemade funeral plans and watching him turn into a vampire, slumbering in a coffin each night.

I'd signed up for an inexpensive cremation with a likable renegade whom I trusted to deliver me to the warehouse door and put me in a homemade pine box for the short trip to the oven. The ashes would be brought back to my family and stashed until the scattering. Who knows, there might even be a burial in the backyard. Surprise me. But in a plastic box? A store-bought urn? No, I still wanted something handmade and personal. Why not the maple tree? Wouldn't it be cosmically balanced to turn our relationship inside out? A chunk of maple fated for the ash heap becomes an urn for ashes instead. *Fire*wood.

THE PLAN is to mount the wood and turn both ends so they're parallel and smooth enough to carve straight-on, then bore out the urn and lop off a slab for a lid. The Wood Turner turns on the lathe and the log lurches into action, spinning like a fishing reel with a whale on the line. The lathe bucks hard and its legs rear off the floor. I back up fast and the Wood Turner flicks off the motor.

"You ever done this before?" I ask.

"Yeah, for wheel hubs on a wagon." He's serious. He explains that he does occasional work for a homestead museum, antique repairs, restorations. Once again I seem to have reversed the clock and dropped into a long-gone time zone. You don't see many computers in the funeral underground, and people aren't in a big hurry. What's the rush? The Wood Turner may not be an official member of that underground, but this is a place where the dead come to be transformed, even if they're only trees. As in the funeral business, this is a kind of alchemy.

The Wood Turner says that the problem here is that we're turning an elliptical chunk of wood with the bark still on, which makes it as wobbly as an unbalanced car wheel. He unscrews the stock, realigns the wood, and switches the drive pulley to a big, orange wheel to slow down the speed. He hands me a plastic face mask and puts one on himself. When he drops the mask he looks like a medieval knight, long hair, bearded and stocky, wielding a chisel instead of a javelin. He props the chisel on an iron bar and gently drives the blade into one end of the spinning wood. The air explodes with wood chips and a high-pitched scraping sound, like a burning brake shoe. When the end is trued up he cuts the motor, turns the wood around, and pares down the other end. He removes the wood and screws a steel faceplate to one end.

While he's adjusting the log, he asks me where I live, and when I tell him, he pauses for a moment and then grins. "Sure, there's an old elm tree on the corner, with a big burl about ten feet up the trunk." He tells me that's how he knows the valley, according to a tree map he keeps in his head, plotted on motorcycle trips scouting for hardwood blowdowns and burls. That's where the logs on his lawn come from, seasoning like fine cheeses before they're cut open.

Between carving sessions, a friend of the Wood Turner's shows up to shoot the breeze. He's a small, gray-haired, older guy, and the Wood Turner introduces him as "a wood worker of the fifth degree," which means he knows his trade. Retired from teaching, he makes his living as a sign maker. When he finds out we're turning an urn he tells me that he once carved his own wooden gravemarker. "But my wife wouldn't let me use it," he shrugs. "She wanted a stone." He says the Veterans' Administration will pay for a stone, but I can see it's not what he wanted.

The Wood Turner shows his friend a new chisel, and they talk about wood and tools and techniques, and they're as happy as a couple of kids playing hooky. That's something I've noticed about wood workers, the pleasure they take, unlike carpenters who put up houses like invading Marines. After a while the old man looks at his watch and says goodbye, raising an imaginary glass to his lips. "Five o'clock," he grins.

The Wood Turner mounts the wood on another lathe set up for turning bowls, and tells me to stand back. "We've screwed into end grain," he warns. "It isn't the greatest stuff to screw into, strength-wise . . . so there's a little potential for . . ." He waves his hand like a log flying through the air. I take an extra step back. He turns on the lathe and the wood starts spinning. Then he picks up a large chisel with a curved scraper on a four-foot wooden handle, props the blade on a support bar in front of the spinning end, and eases the blade into the wood. The chisel howls into the log and a hole begins to appear. He drives the scraper into the maple, pulls it out, removes a hunk of sawdust, and drives it in again. After doing this several times, like a dentist boring out a filling, he cuts the motor and invites me to try it. He tells me to hold the handle under my arm, rest the scraper on the bar, and drive the tip in.

"You've worked with a hand plane?" he asks.

I nod.

"The bevel is just like a hand plane, a low-angle block. The grab can be bad if you're not careful. The idea is to rub your bevel flat. The lower edge is low down, you want this parallel to whatever you're cutting. If you get up too high, it's grabby, it wants to dig in, which makes it really ticklish."

I imagine myself impaled on a chisel as big as a canoe paddle while carving my own funeral urn. Talk about tempting fate. I wonder if I've paid enough attention to the self-destructive dimension of this strange odyssey. I imagine the *National Inquirer* headline—"He Tried to Chisel the Undertaker out of His Fee"—and then I clamp the handle tight under my arm and drive the blade into the wood. The scraper throbs in my hands and the blade squeals like a stuck pig. Wood chips ricochet off my face mask, and I can feel the chisel handle trying to lift me off the floor. The scraper drills deeper into the dark hole until I hit bottom, pull back, and drive it in again. The world boils down to this pulsing rhythm, the sweet green wood opening up sensuously, pushing back and giving, until it's done.

The Wood Turner cuts the motor and the wood stops spinning and we examine the urn. There's a six-inch-diameter boring to within a couple of inches of the bottom. I can't carve any deeper or I'll smash into the screws holding the face plate. He asks me if I want to make a pedestal for the base.

"A pedestal?"

"You've got the contrast of the organic wood and the turned object," he points out, "but right now you wouldn't know it was a turned object."

"You think it's too rustic?"

"It's up to you."

I see his point. It still looks like a chunk of firewood. "Okay, let's get something going here."

"That's the whole idea," he says, grinning. "Play around, play with everything you do."

The Wood Turner tells me that taking more wood off the bottom will prevent cracking as the wood dries. "Anytime you have less material on end grain, you're more apt to not split. Any place we can get rid of volume in this piece, what cracks we have shouldn't get any more massive." He runs a circle of packing tape around the bottom, above where he intends to carve, to prevent the bark from shattering. "You want a lumped foot? A beaded foot? A rounded foot that looks kind of like a doughnut?"

I imagine the urn balanced on a soggy doughnut and shake my head. "How about something crisp?"

He flips on the switch and the wood revs up. He adjusts the bar so he can carve from the side, picks up a smaller chisel, and drives the steel into the wood. Bark flies, sapwood appears, and soon there's a one-inch pedestal at the base. It's angled out about forty-five degrees, like the nozzles you see on the bottom of a space shuttle. The Wood Turner cuts the motor and removes the urn and stands it up on the bench.

"It's a little bit of an oriental flair," he suggests.

"Or a tree with a rocket."

We both laugh, and then he mounts the urn on another lathe, carves a line for the lid, and uses an electric chainsaw to lop it off. Then it's back to the lathe, where he turns a mortise so the lid will sit securely on the urn.

"How about a handle?" he asks. You might want to use it as a cookie jar."

Now we're cooking. I suggest something to echo the pedestal, and he carves a slope into the top of the lid, topped off with an angular knob. I take off the lid. To me, it's beginning to look like the Holy Grail.

I wish we had a bottle of champagne to try it out.

The Wood Turner gives me some suggestions on how to season the urn with a minimum of cracking. He recommends a thick coat of Butcher's Wax and then a couple of months in the cellar wrapped up in a brown paper bag. "That'll slow down the drying, move the moisture out as slow as possible. I'm not guaranteeing how it'll work out. Remember, it's dead green."

I ask the Wood Turner what I owe him.

"A fifty dollar bill. That's what I charge for a half-day training workshop."

Sounds fair. Woodworking school, last stop on the Deadsville Express. Hasn't that been the whole point of this trip? To learn something new. Or perhaps it's something old, fading, nearly forgotten? The art of facing death. And what about the Wood Turner's advice to play, play with everything you do? I think that's what I've been doing too, turning my fear of death into a horror comedy melodrama, a one-man *Totentanz*.

It's raining and dark as I drive off into the night with the urn on the seat beside me. On the news they're playing Mariachi music, a story from

Mexico. Feasts have been prepared, the favorite food and drink of the departed, to be carried to the cemeteries in celebration *El Dia del Muerto*, the Day of the Dead. It's a couple of days after Halloween, and throughout North and South America there's been a cross-continental orgy of macabre revelry, Halloween, All Saint's Day, All Soul's Day, spirits conjured and spirits mourned. But it's really a time of celebrating the astonishing fact of being alive, not dead, and bragging like hell about it. Forget the sanctimonious humility and the trembling fear of death. Get drunk, get laid, revel in being on the right side of the grass. As Ethan Allen said, "Goddamn 'em, let the angels wait."

LAST WORDS An unseasonable late night autumn thunderstorm rolls over the mountains and the radio crackles with static. Two scientists discuss geriatric research and medical technology. The genetic code is about to crack. "If you can hang on for another fifty years, the human life span will be extended ten-fold," one predicts. Lightning sizzles through the speakers like sulphur matches struck on sandpaper. Seven hundred, eight hundred, a thousand years. They don't say anything about how those years will be parceled out. Forty years in high school? Nine centuries of senior citizenship? A midlife crisis two hundred years long? The storm moves closer. I wonder how the Age of Agelessness will affect funeral workers. Will it put them out of business, or, after a taste of life everlasting, will we finally, gratefully, give the undertakers all the love and affection they've been missing? The Greeks told of Aurora's husband, Tithonus, who was granted immortality by Zeus. Alas, it was not specified that he remain young, and so he grew older and older, unable to die. His mind went and his body shrank, until he was a babbling imbecile. Finally, Aurora took pity and put him out of his misery. She turned him into a grasshopper.

CHELSEA GREEN

Sustainable living has many facets. Chelsea Green's celebration of the sustainable arts has led us to publish trend-setting books about organic gardening, solar electricity and renewable energy, innovative building techniques, regenerative forestry, local and bioregional democracy, and whole foods. The company's published works, while intensely practical, are also entertaining and inspirational, demonstrating that an ecological approach to life is consistent with producing beautiful, eloquent, and useful books, videos, and audio cassettes.

For more information about Chelsea Green, or to request a free catalog, call toll-free (800) 639-4099, or write to us at P.O. Box 428, White River Junction, Vermont 05001. Visit our Web site at www.chelseagreen.com.

Chelsea Green's titles include:

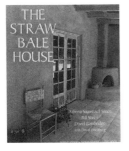

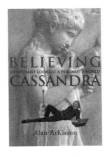